HORIZON

NOVEMBER, 1961 · VOLUME IV, NUMBER 2

l'Horlogere.　　　Die Uhrmacherin.

1. Une pendule. 1. eine Kasten Uhr. 2. montre de repedition. 2. eine Repetier Sack
Uhr. 3. montre emboetée. 3. eine Stock Uhr.

HORIZON

A Magazine of the Arts

NOVEMBER, 1961 · *VOLUME IV, NUMBER 2*

PUBLISHER
James Parton

EDITORIAL DIRECTOR
Joseph J. Thorndike, Jr.

EDITOR
William Harlan Hale

ASSOCIATE EDITOR
Ralph Backlund

ASSISTANT EDITORS
Ada Pesin
Jane Wilson

CONTRIBUTING EDITOR
Margery Darrell

EDITORIAL ASSISTANTS
Shirley Abbott, Caroline Backlund
Wendy Buehr, Alan Doré

COPY EDITOR
Mary Ann Pfeiffer
Assistants: Joan Rehe, Ruth H. Wolfe

ART DIRECTOR
Irwin Glusker
Associate Art Director: Elton Robinson

ADVISORY BOARD
Gilbert Highet, *Chairman*
Frederick Burkhardt   Oliver Jensen
Marshall B. Davidson   Jotham Johnson
Richard M. Ketchum   John Walker

EUROPEAN CONSULTING EDITOR
J. H. Plumb
Christ's College, Cambridge

EUROPEAN BUREAU
Gertrudis Feliu, *Chief*
28 Quai du Louvre, Paris

HORIZON is published every two months by American Heritage Publishing Co., Inc. Executive and editorial offices: 551 Fifth Ave., New York 17, N.Y. HORIZON welcomes contributions but can assume no responsibility for unsolicited material.

All correspondence about subscriptions should be addressed to: HORIZON Subscription Office, 379 West Center St., Marion, Ohio.

Single Copies: $4.50
Annual Subscriptions: $21.00 in the U.S. & Can.
$22.00 elsewhere

An annual index is published every September, priced at $1. HORIZON is also indexed in the *Readers Guide to Periodical Literature.*

Title registered U.S. Patent Office
Second-class postage paid at New York, N.Y.

COVER: Paul Klee had the kind of innocent magic that could evoke a wistful human face from the simplest of geometric forms. In *Senecio* he does it with circles for head and eyes, a straight line to suggest a nose, and two tiny rectangles where one would expect a mouth. "It is not my task to reproduce appearances," he once wrote in his diary; "for that there is the photographic plate . . . but my faces are truer than life." *Senecio* (now in the Kunstmuseum in Basel) was painted in 1922, a year or so after Klee had entered upon a happy decade of teaching at the Bauhaus in Germany. This was the revolutionary school of design created by Walter Gropius; in its artistic ferment— to which Klee contributed—were born the ideas that have since influenced everything from advertising to architecture. An article on the Bauhaus begins on page 58.

FRONTISPIECE: *L'Horlogère*—the Watchmaker's Wife—is a German engraving from the eighteenth century, when such conceits were popular. Called "trades engravings," they purported to show how various tradespeople might look if only they dressed the part. Thus the *jardinier* and his *jardinière* would be decked out in fruit and vegetables (one of these appears in HORIZON for May, 1959). The watchmaker's wife has her head and bust encased in a pedestal clock which narrows down at exactly the right moment to give her an elegantly cinched-in waist. Her skirt is a rococo table model, and in her hand she holds a repeater watch—a type that sounded the hours and quarter-hours with a pleasant chime. These are all good examples of eighteenth-century timepieces.

PICASSO
AND HIS PUBLIC

Which Picasso? As great an impresario as he is a painter, Picasso in his lifetime has produced a whole repertory of artists bearing the same name, each of one distinct style and period. Never has an artist so commanded his audience through his dazzling changes, or attained such Old Masters' prices while yet alive

If Pablo Picasso is the greatest single figure in the artistic upheaval of the twentieth century, he is no less a landmark in the changing relationship between the painter and his public. In the long history of art, perhaps no master has ever basked in the sunshine of such esteem while yet alive as this insurgent of our generation—or rather of almost two generations. Probably none except Rembrandt, Michelangelo, and Leonardo da Vinci has been the subject of so many scholarly books and monographs. Certainly no painter in his own lifetime has been prized so highly in sheer money terms as this prolific octogenarian, whose *Les Baladins* of 1905 (shown on the opposite page) was purchased two years ago by the Staatsgalerie at Stuttgart for one million marks ($250,000).

The love affair between Picasso and his public, to say nothing of his market, represents the culmination of the century-long process of change in the world of art patronage. Before the French Revolution brought a sudden end to the eighteenth century, a tight little circle of artists lived in a close relationship with their patrons, usually royal, or at least of the nobility. There was no question or need of publicity for the artist, scarcely even of a dealer (for royal commissions were granted directly through the proper court authorities); most important, there was no problem of public approval. Since the king and his nobility could do no wrong, certainly in terms of social recognition of the arts, they could, if they wished, patronize an unknown, unfashionable artist, even a radical innovator, without any of the embarrassment that a Pittsburgh steel magnate or a Hollywood producer would feel were he to eschew the current fashion for "name" artists and hang his walls with either old-fashioned-

looking conservatives or unconventional young painters.

Such a state of mind and of society existed as early as the fifteenth century, when a gangster-condottiere like Federigo da Montefeltro was unconventional enough to become the patron of an unknown *hors-série* master named Piero della Francesca for the decoration, now immortal, of his palaces and churches. In the eighteenth century Frederick the Great of Prussia broke away from tawdry Hohenzollern taste and the bumpkinish showiness of his countrified nobility to send his emissaries to Paris so that he could become a collector of Watteau, Pater, and Lancret (and, in fact, of Voltaire as well). Later, even the great onsurge of popular leveling-down following the fall of the Bastille, and the publicity apparatus that went with it, did not immediately engulf all Europe. In the less urbane courts there were royal figures who, through the end of the nineteenth century, did not care a fig about pleasing the public or whether the artists they liked and patronized were riding on a tide of high-priced public applause: an outstanding example is, of course, King Ludwig II of Bavaria and his backing of the music of Richard Wagner at a time when it was vehemently unpopular. The

This poetic painting, done during Picasso's Circus period in 1905, was bought recently by the state museum in Stuttgart, Germany, for the equivalent of $250,000—the highest price ever paid for the work of a living painter. Les Baladins ("the traveling actors") embodies the mournful mood and classic serenity of this period of the artist's work. The museum received a bonus in the form of an earlier painting done on the reverse side of the canvas (see next page).

By ALFRED FRANKFURTER

A typical Blue period painting,
Femme Assise au Capuchon *was
done in 1902 when Picasso was
twenty-one and very poor. Even
three years later, when he painted*
Les Baladins *on its reverse side, he
was still poor enough to need to
use the same canvas over again.*

prices paid by the Paris agent of Frederick the Great, Jean de Julienne, for those Watteaus and Lancrets in the 1720's and 1730's have not all been recorded (the Prussian king owed nobody an accounting for his expenditures), but we know that two or three of them cost about $1,000 apiece. (One of the Watteaus, received by the late Kaiser Wilhelm II as part of a property settlement between his family and the Prussian state, was sold a few years ago to the Royal Museum in Stockholm for $275,000.)

Watteau had been made into a recognizable public "image," of course, by two centuries of adulation and critical publication—the machinery for which exists as practically and universally for artists and works of art in the twentieth century as it does for movie stars and brand names. And the truly signal difference between the artist-public relationship of a century ago and the present lies in the utilization of that machinery with intelligence and virtuosity for the benefit of living artists. The prices paid at recent sales, including that of the Stuttgart Picasso, recall a celebrated bon mot of Degas's. Near the end of his life the painter saw—or would have seen, had he not by then been blind—one of his can-

vases, the famous *Danseuses à la barre,* sold at auction for approximately $95,000. Forty years earlier he had been paid $200 for it by the man whose collection was being sold. Asked how he felt, Degas replied: "I feel exactly like the horse that has just won the Grand Prix and sees the cup being handed to the jockey."

There is, of course, no true parallel here. Picasso is still painting and Degas, perforce, was not. Moreover, Degas possessed only a handful of important pictures from his own hand, while Picasso is the owner of the largest collection of Picassos in the world.

What is most astonishing, in the case of Picasso, is that such regal market prices should have been attained by an artist while still in high production and thus adding constantly to his available work. This itself is already all but immeasurable. The cumulative catalogue of Picasso's output, *Les Oeuvres de Picasso,* edited in close collaboration with Picasso himself by his friend and Boswell, the Greek-born art critic Christian Zervos, lists in its eleven volumes so far published, a total of 6,751 works executed from 1895 through 1944 (of which slightly more than half are finished pictures

6

in oils, gouache, or other media and the remainder are drawings). But this leaves all the work of Picasso's immensely creative years since 1944 still unaccounted for. What is the total of his works since then? No one knows; it surely amounts to additional thousands. And now comes another friend of Picasso's, the American author-photographer David Douglas Duncan, to illustrate in a sumptuous new book, *Picasso's Picassos: The Treasures of La Californie,* the vastness of the artist's private collection of his own work.

Mr. Duncan presents 103 color plates and another 530 black-and-white reproductions of individual works presently in Picasso's own possession, many of which have not heretofore been publicly exhibited.* Yet this by no means exhausts the entirety of Picasso's holdings, which Duncan estimates as including perhaps 550 pictures stored in the master's spacious villa of La Californie at Cannes (most of them stacked five and six deep, facing the walls) and another 500 or more recently transported to Picasso's newer establishment, the fifteenth-century Château de Vauvenargues, in the fastnesses of the Midi. All of Picasso's successive periods and styles are represented in either collection, and there is no dearth of paintings from his now particularly sought-after years (1895 to 1907). Even at that time, despite his eagerness to gain a public, Picasso seems to have held back a number of his favorite canvases; in more recent years, he has been in the market to buy back some of his early works.

It is tempting to speculate on the material worth of the estate in pictures which this founder-master of the School of Paris is likely to leave. Yet an accurate estimate is almost impossible. There are 532 paintings catalogued in the Duncan book; even if these were, say, a collection of 532 drawings by Michelangelo, it would take perhaps ten years of the most judicious expert management to sell so many and still realize their individual market value. If, however, we may be allowed to assume that in some fashion all these Picassos could be sold, one by one, at their present market value, they ought to be worth upwards of $10,000,000. By the same kind of calculation, the total value of all the Picassos in existence should be somewhere in the neighborhood of $100,000,000.

What makes Picasso unique in the history of art is the degree to which he has become what may be described as an orchestrater of the public attitude toward his work, expertly creating sympathetic responses to his various successive styles. These changes of style, as all followers of his art know, are so distinct that each has been endowed with a name of its own: there is the Blue period of 1901–1904, the Circus period of 1905, the Rose period of 1905–1906, the Negroid period of 1907–1908, the Analytical Cubist period of 1909–1912, the Synthetic Cubist period of 1913–1921, the Classical period of 1920–1924, the Metamorphic period of 1925–1930, the Bone period of 1929, the Stained Glass period of 1932, the monochrome-linear period of *Guernica* of 1937

* An early glimpse into Picasso's collection of his own works was provided in Mr. Duncan's portfolio, "Picasso's Lady," in HORIZON, for January, 1960.

and after—and so on. In a remark that may be apocryphal yet remains symptomatic, Picasso is said to have answered someone's criticism, "I don't like Picasso," with the response, "Which Picasso?"

There have been a few isolated instances of an artist effectively promoting his art to his patrons—such as Titian's long sales correspondence with King Philip II of Spain, persuading that great Catholic monarch to accept allegories violently modern to him, including even nudes, which however classical and symbolical, were totally unlike anything that a still medieval Spain had ever known or seen.* Yet in Picasso it demanded a man who was as great an impresario as an artist to make his own protean changes in style understood and accepted. Why did he undertake them? It would surely have been far easier for him to continue to do what most artists have done; namely, once having found a style germane to him and increasingly accepted by his audience, to have retained it, always merely expanding its possibilities without making such abrupt and radical changes as he did. For instance, there was the break from the eloquently lyrical Blue and Rose periods, which clearly proclaimed their intensely modern derivation from the figures of Greek vases, to the sharp-edged distortions of his Negroid period, born out of the jagged contours of primitive African sculpture.

None of Picasso's numerous interpreters have offered explanations for such a sudden shift other than his own restless exploratory nature—which, to be sure, he has since demonstrated time and time again. But to one who has specialized in the history of style it seems as if there were other motives present than simply passionate exploration by an artist of one new stylistic dialect after another.

It looks rather as though Picasso has always been, like a playwright, constantly "in dialogue" with his audience, ever needing the audience, sensing it and feeling it out like a lover pursuing the object of his affections. He has been, in many ways, like a *metteur en scène,* a scenic designer, who phrases his plays in a new language yet always captures the heretofore hidden forms which lie in the dream world of his public and materializes them for that public. In this century, saturated with a new and continually changing series of visual experiences, such a scenic master has helped both create and reflect the visual restlessness of his public.

As to the effect of his changing "periods" on his public and hence on his market, there is the discerning remark of his sometime Paris dealer, the late Paul Rosenberg: "Picasso has had the good sense, of all artists, to die at least eight times"; which is to say that each of his "periods" is as closed a book—in terms of supply and demand—as if it represented the lifetime output of a single artist. His mind and his artistic being have changed so completely with each new phase he has invented that retrogression would be as impossible for him as for Edison to have gone back from the incandescent lamp to the oil lamp. Despite his enormous output over almost six decades, each of his phases

* For a discussion of Philip II, see H. R. Trevor-Roper's "The Two Spains of Don Quixote," on pages 106–113 of this issue of HORIZON.

Blue Period, 1901–1904   *Circus Period, 1905*   *Rose Period, 1905–1906*   *Negroid Period, 1907–1908*

The best-known periods of Picasso's painting range from 1901 to around 1930. Although the artist has never stopped producing prolifically, his later work does not fall into such sharply differentiated styles. His most sought-after periods are represented above by outstanding examples in American collections. Left to right: The Old Guitarist, *1903 (Art Institute of Chicago);* Family of Saltimbanques, *1905 (National Gallery of*

remains, in effect, a limited edition: the fact that there can never be any more canvases of his early Blue period may help to explain why the most important of those extant now easily sell at six-figure prices. Some of his more recent styles have not yet approached anything like this summit, and sometimes it is a little difficult for the lay public—especially hardheaded businessmen possessing the kind of cash required to buy a "Blue Picasso" nowadays—to grasp the absoluteness with which each period has come to an end. There is the story of one sagacious New York manufacturer who, just about ready the other day to buy a Blue period work for the more than a hundred thousand dollars asked for it, demanded a little guardedly: "Why shouldn't Picasso paint another 'Blue' picture at this price if he can get only $10,000 for one in his current style?"

The phenomenal results of Picasso's approach—a new model every few years, and a refusal or inability to reproduce last year's—stand out particularly when compared to the values placed on early works of some of his renowned contemporaries, men whose development followed a more continuous course. Though major works of Henri Matisse at the height of his maturity have recently brought as much as $150,000, canvases of his youthful twenties still hover in the neighborhood of $30,000.

Picasso's stylistic leaps and bounds have made it hard for him over sixty years with his critics, who repeatedly have just about grown ready to accept, and found the language to interpret, one style when the artist has suddenly flabbergasted them with a new one. Thus, his critical corpus has almost always remained at least one lap behind him, which makes his speedy acceptance by a public willing to pay to prove it even more remarkable. Now we have all around us a visual world that has been formed literally in the image of Picasso. Even today's academicians and other conservatives have adopted those tall, cadaverous, melancholy, El Greco-ish figures of the Blue period, now a half-century old; there is scarcely a fashion or department-store advertisement that does not reflect the architectonic organization of Picasso's Cubism; political caricature abroad leans on the violent expressionist drawing of the twentieth century's great antiwar painting, *Guernica*. The artist has not merely educated but virtually *immersed* his public in his own forms as has no other artist in history—for never before have newly invented visual forms passed so rapidly from the studio into popular art.

It was, however, not always thus. If the prices paid for an artist's paintings are in fact a guide to his aesthetic rank, Picasso before World War I may be said to have had no more than a *succès d'estime*. His first important dealer, Daniel-Henry Kahnweiler, a perceptive German of Jewish extraction, who in the years before World War I

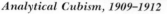

Analytical Cubism, 1909–1912   *Synthetic Cubism, 1913–21*   *Classical Period, 1920–1924*   *Metamorphic Period, 1925–1930*

Art, Washington, Chester Dale Collection); Woman with Loaves, *1905 (Philadelphia Museum of Art);* Les Demoiselles D'Avignon, *1907 (Museum of Modern Art);* Portrait of Kahnweiler, *1910 (Art Institute of Chicago);* The Dog and Cock, *1921 (Collection the late Stephen C. Clark);* Woman in White, *1923 (Metropolitan Museum of Art, from The Museum of Modern Art);* Seated Woman, *1927 (Coll. J. T. Soby).*

established a small gallery on the Left Bank, recalls that the "first buyers of Cubist Picasso were Hermann Rupf, Wilhelm Uhde [both also German residents in Paris], Vincent Kramar, and Roger Dutilleul. The prices were very low then—a few hundred francs, but they rose afterward, slowly yet steadily."

Most of his early purchasers were writers and poets; among them was Hugo von Hofmannsthal, the Viennese poet who wrote the libretto for Richard Strauss's *Der Rosenkavalier* and who spent his first royalty check from that opera for two Picassos about 1911. "Then," Picasso's dealer recalls, "came the 'Kahnweiler sales,' and prices collapsed entirely." Those sales were postwar auctions held by the French custodian of enemy property who had confiscated the paintings in this German citizen's gallery. In 1921–23 several hundred Picassos were thrown on the market at forced sales. Picasso's tiny gouache of 1903, *The Harlequin's Family,* which brought only 600 francs (then about $45) at a Kahnweiler enemy-property sale in 1921, was to be resold at auction at Sotheby's in London thirty-eight years later for £12,000 ($33,600).

As the artist marched from style to style, each time making news as he concluded one and boldly introduced another, the tide of his acceptance gathered astonishing and irresistible force. His major painting of 1905, *The Family of Saltimbanques,* was first bought from him in 1908 for the equivalent of $200; in 1931 Chester Dale bought it for more than the equivalent of $40,000 and later deposited it on permanent loan in the National Gallery in Washington. An early Picasso pencil and water-color poster, *Au Moulin Rouge,* was auctioned at Parke-Bernet in New York in 1950 for $1,650 and then again ten years later for $47,500: a 3,000 per cent rise in value in a decade, and a small fortune for—a poster.

"Museums," Picasso remarked disdainfully in the 1930's, "are just a lot of lies, and people who make art their business are mostly imposters. Everyone wants to understand art. Why not try to understand the song of a bird? Why do people love the night, a flower, everything around them without trying to understand them? Whereas painting, they wish to understand." For all that, Picasso owes more to museums than his blast would indicate. The solid foundation of his public place began to be laid after about 1910 by the German, Swiss, and Scandinavian institutions that were among his first large collectors. The family portrait on the grass (see pages 10–11), which now belongs to the Musée des Beaux Arts in Liège, Belgium, was originally purchased in 1913 by the Wallraf-Richartz Museum in Cologne, Germany. There it remained until 1938 when Hitler in his campaign to purge Germany of "degenerate art"—as he called almost all of modern art—had it exhibited in Munich as part of an intended chamber of horrors, after which, along with other modern works forced out of German museums, it was

9

sold at auction in Switzerland, on the eve of war in 1939 for $15,000. It would easily bring more than $100,000 today.

The greatest museum representations of all are those in Moscow and Leningrad—thanks to two pre-Soviet industrialists who were among Picasso's earliest and heaviest purchasers before 1914. Nobody has ever successfully explained how these apparently quite typical businessmen, Shchukine and Morosov, came so early to recognize Picasso's genius, but the evidence remains in Russia. Sequestered by the Soviet government, the collection has been divided between the museums in Moscow and Leningrad.

The Blue period has perhaps done better in terms of material appreciation than any other of Picasso's styles, although more recent sophisticated critical appraisal, tending toward current taste for abstraction, ranks his Analytical Cubist period (1909–1912) higher and finds the Blue period subjects somewhat old-fashionedly anecdotal and sentimental. Almost comparable in rise to the Blue paintings are those of the briefer and rarer Rose period of 1905–1906. The succeeding Negroid works are far less expensive nowadays than those of the Rose period, even though they were the first Picassos to meet with acclaim in their time from avant-garde critics in both Europe and America. It was the historic Armory Show in 1913, which really brought Picasso en bloc to the attention of American painters, critics, and collectors. By that time, of course, the artist had been deeply engaged for several years in his exploration of Cubism. One of his earliest works in that revolutionary style, *The Girl with a Mandolin* of 1909, was sold a few years ago by Picasso's friend, critic, and early purchaser, Roland Penrose of London, to Governor Nelson Rockefeller for $100,000. Since then, other important works of this not readily legible style, executed almost like geometric architectural diagrams in thin brownish pigment, have sold for between $150,000 and $175,000. (In the disastrous Kahnweiler auctions in 1921–23 their prices averaged about $500.)

A key to the later Synthetic Cubist period is its masterpiece, the *Three Musicians* (page 13), purchased for the Museum of Modern Art in 1949 for what may have been

Picasso's engaging family portrait, The Soler Family Lunching on the Grass, *was painted in 1903 during his Blue period, when he took portrait commissions to help make a living. Originally it had a background of grass and trees painted by another artist because Picasso did not have time to finish it. By 1913, when it was sold to the Cologne museum, Picasso had replaced the landscape with the present blue background. During Hitler's campaign to rid German museums of what he considered "degenerate art," the painting was banned and sold in Switzerland in 1939 for $15,000 to the museum in Liège, Belgium. Today it would easily be worth $100,000.*

about $90,000. With its other version in the Gallatin Collection in the Philadelphia Museum, it stands out today as perhaps the most immediately popular and pleasing as well as the most influential of all Picasso's works in terms of design. If it were on the market, it is reasonable to suppose it could bring as much as $500,000.

The succeeding Classical period—maybe, paradoxically, because its tranquil Neo-Greek figures were so readily understandable and thus seemed a step back from Picasso's frontier—has never been either a collector's or critic's high favorite. Hence the Metropolitan Museum's acquisition in about 1951 of the popular *Woman in White* for some $50,000 may represent about the highest price that paintings of this style are likely to bring.

With Picasso's paintings of the early 1930's—some of them based on stained-glass experiments and devoted to extreme, convoluted forms—we enter a new phase of difficulty. Indeed this phase, represented for instance by the Modern Museum's famous *Girl before a Mirror* of 1932, probably remains the most difficult of all Picasso's styles for the public as well as his critics to comprehend. Here the artist's injunction against the effort to "wish to understand" strikes home with especial force. Valentine Dudensing, one of the shrewdest dealers in modern art New York ever knew and the man who sold the *Girl* to the Museum, himself echoed Picasso by remarking, "I never can sell a picture I understand. If I fully understand it, I feel its day is already over—that we've already digested its ideas and there's no future in it."

Paintings of Picasso's succeeding years and styles, particularly since 1940, cannot be chronicled or assessed in quite the same terms as those that come before. This is either because of our short perspective of time on them or because of the effect the rise in esteem of earlier Picassos has automatically had on the reception of later ones as they have come off the easel. At no time since the end of World War II has a freshly painted Picasso been greeted with less than unanimous acclaim by leading critics—none of them wished to take a chance on being proven wrong, as were some of their predecessors of a generation ago. Nor has any been sold for less than the range of $12,000–$25,000 for a fair-sized canvas. These figures demonstrate, however, that despite the immense prestige and acceptance which the artist now holds, the work of his most recent years has not yet found financial favor comparable to that of his earlier ones.

These later paintings remind us how great a span of time and ideas in the history of art—indeed of the world—Picasso bridges. His Blue period dates from his first arrival in Paris around 1900, in the wake of Toulouse-Lautrec, and its *raison d'être* grows out of the prevailing impressionist and postimpressionist aesthetic of *"l'art pour l'art."* But any art-for-art's-sake premise was dismissed by Picasso, at the very latest, by the period commencing with *Guernica* in 1937. From the moment that the German planes bombed the women and children of this undefended town, Picasso became a "committed" artist. The problems of the world became the problems of his art, as they did for his idol Goya during the Napoleonic Wars: not alone murder from the sky, horribly premonitive though it has come to be today; also the cruelty of man to other living beings, seen in girls throttling chickens and corn-cobbed peasants brandishing the bloody spears of picadors. It is hard to believe that these subjects can ever rival, in the favor of collectors anxious to decorate their penthouses, the operatically tragic harlequins of the Blue period or the tan mosaics, bearing snatches of popular songs, of the Analytical Cubist period.

Yet in the most recent years the evaluation of Picasso's latter-day output has again become subject to change—for the better. In March, 1958, a not particularly significant *Seated Woman,* dated June, 1941, brought £8,000 ($22,400), presumably at least 50 per cent more than the price at which it had changed hands in France during the war years.

What will happen henceforth? Are the art speculators, who at least in France are numerous, correct in supposing that Picasso's later paintings—say after 1928—will have a rise in value comparable to that of the earlier ones? It is hard to say: there seems to be in these paintings at least as much competence, if by no means as much artistic invention, as in the world-shaking innovations from 1900 through about 1925.

The relationship between an artist and his admirers is often established elsewhere than in the auction room or the dealer's gallery. It is perhaps nearest the truth to say that the true repute of Picasso, like that of almost all painters since 1850, is established by living fellow artists, ever the most severe judges of their peers. It is the good new painting of one's own day that creates the current visual climate for masters of the past, even those of only yesterday.

What of the future? Few octogenarian artists (except perhaps Titian) have lived to see their ideas and forms still valid currency among younger artists. Even Renoir, guiding star of impressionism until his death in 1919 at the age of seventy-eight, saw Picasso's comet flash twenty years before and unsay most of what he had stated in his life. No single younger successor to Picasso has yet been seen high enough in the sky to mean anything. Yet the movement called "abstract expressionism," born fifteen years ago in New York, has launched a wave of free-form painting across the world, not least in Picasso's Paris and Picasso's Spain. Its license of form, and absence of subject matter, derives much more from the expressionist tendencies of Matisse than from the always controlled form and decisive themes of Picasso. Out of such rumblings often come the earthquakes of artistic displacement. Nothing like this has begun to happen yet. It is well to remember, however, that a king reigns only until a new one is on the throne.

Alfred Frankfurter, Editor of Art News, *is a prominent student of the history of art and of the world art market.*

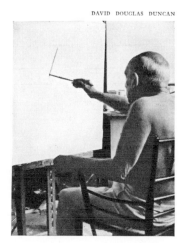

Because Three Musicians, *painted in 1921, is probably the most popular of Picasso's paintings, it might sell today for $500,000, the price of a fine Ingres portrait sold recently.* Three Musicians *is considered one of Picasso's masterpieces and is his outstanding work in the decorative style of Synthetic Cubism. His subject is a triumvirate from the Italian commedia dell' arte: at left, Pierrot with a dog; in the center, Harlequin; at right, a mysterious monk. His searching, still youthful look in those years appears in the Man Ray photograph at far left, taken at forty-two; next, David Douglas Duncan's camera observes the master in our own day.*

The New Face of

BRITAIN

A Portfolio of Photographs by Bruce Davidson

The girl on the facing page was photographed this year on a London street. She bears certain marks of her nationality—love of animals, love of nature—but her general appearance would scarcely serve to identify her as a Briton of the ancient breed. She is in fact a member of a new generation which fits no stereotype yet recognizable to foreign eyes.

The picture was taken by Bruce Davidson, a young American photographer who has won distinction in recent years as a photo-reporter of American society, most notably with a pictorial essay on a teen-age gang in Brooklyn. He went to England with no preconceptions and no special assignment, but with a keenly sensitive photographic eye.

Traveling through England and Scotland, he recorded many sights of traditional Britain: the duke at his castle, the sheepherder on his moor, the banker in his City. But his eye was caught, too, by the scenes of a newer Britain, the Britain of the welfare state and the vanishing empire, of Jimmy Porter and the red-brick universities, of peace marchers and teddy boys and *Room at the Top*.

Is this the true composite image of modern Britain? For another view HORIZON turned to a distinguished English man of letters, Alan Pryce-Jones. As editor of the London *Times Literary Supplement,* Mr. Pryce-Jones viewed England for many years from the inner citadel of the British Establishment. During the past year he has been in the United States, studying and writing about the American cultural world, and is thus qualified to judge both the British scene and Mr. Davidson's interpretation of it. His article, on the following pages, precedes a portfolio of Davidson photographs.

"But cheerfulness keeps breaking in..."

Fog. It is the word which is first evoked—unjustly, on the whole—by the idea of England. The fault is largely Dickens's. That famous opening chapter of *Bleak House* has set the tone for all time. Fog in the Thames; fog creeping into a green aura of gaslight; fog giving an extra edge to the overall smell of gin and acetylene: such is the emotional symbol which still represents English life to the outside world.

And it is true that England remains in spirit a nineteenth-century island. There may at last be one surprising skyscraper to lift its head above the roof line of St. James's Palace; there may be one modern road, but even that leads to the most Gladstonian of British cities, Birmingham; there may be less gin and more sunlight. All the same, there are great tracts of England over which Queen Victoria still reigns.

It is therefore all the more fascinating to observe the England of Bruce Davidson. Here is a brilliant young photographer, who has already brought a searching eye to bear on the New World, assessing the Old. He has seen what it takes an acute eye to see: that under a surface which reflects the influence of social and international change, the old England persists. Continental and American pressures have been linked to a spirit of self-renewal that has kept the British on their toes, but they have managed to assault the twentieth century without quite cutting adrift from the past. They may have overdone this conservatism. Thus, what fires Mr. Davidson's imagination is the world of a recent film, *Saturday Night and Sunday Morning*. He responds to the gasworks, the back-to-back slum cottages, the stained glass in a pub window, the wilting fern in an *art nouveau* pot as keenly as to the new beatniks and the Ban-the-Bomb movement.

There are other Englands, however, and I should not wish all of them to be forgotten. There is the England of the Midlands, for instance. A poet has called them "sodden and unkind," and visitors usually pass rapidly through to the West or the North without stopping to look. Were they to pause, they would see a microcosm of the firm center which keeps English life in trim through all the vicissitudes of society. It is the England of Bunyan and Cromwell and Cowper. Landscapes are small and flat, villages still feel the double tug of the parsonage and the manor house. The country gentry are not very exciting, but they are utterly unmoved by such passing phenomena as Mr. K, the cobalt bomb, and massacres in the Congo. Here and there, at the end of avenues, stand the palaces, which lead a peculiar life of their own. Only two kinds of public gain easy access to them: blood relations of the owner, and trippers from the industrial cities with a half crown to spend. For neighbors are not encouraged, except at the annual Conservative fete in the park, at a Hunt Ball, or a coming-of-age. Such palaces may be out-of-date; yet even at the royal palace of Whitehall, in the days of absolute monarchy, the public was encouraged to stare at its betters, so that there is no break with the past in a great house which prefers to welcome its visitors by the busload rather than in social couples.

Then there is the England of East Anglia, of windy skies, driven partridges, churches like small cathedrals serving no community at all, and—most English of occasions—Benjamin Britten's Aldeburgh Festival. This is the England of the North Sea pirates. The speech of the inhabitants is incomprehensible to an outsider, and each village is tightly buttoned into its private life. The mines and factories which have made the Midlands rich seem as remote as Pittsburgh. Again, the Eastern counties form an England of the past, barely touched by the changes of the last generation. But they possess certain qualities of mind and heart which deserve to be commemorated: the solid country qualities which have kept England steady—on the whole—through all the vagaries of an industrial civilization.

I should also have wished to see, among these photographs, more of the West. It is an essential fact about the English that they have constantly been kept up to the mark by their Celtic neighbors. Just as another imperial race, the Austrians, came to count on the industry of the Czechs, the vigor of the Hungarians, and the nervous energy of the Poles to run their country, so the English have drawn on the huge, if often grudging, pool of talent offered them by the Welsh, the Scots, and the Irish. An Englishman has a tendency to slump at his work, but, when he senses a Celtic eye upon him, he squares his shoulders at once. And so I regret the absence of the coombs, the chines, and the moors of the West—the more so because Bruce Davidson has obviously responded eagerly to the opalescent splendors of western Scotland.

But there is one major change in the English life of the last fifteen years, and it is chiefly that which Mr. Davidson might have stressed in his pictures. A feeling for color, for excitement, for life, in fact, has been growing throughout the country ever since the people of Great Britain became tired of poverty and restriction in the years which directly followed the last war. It goes in step with a general increase in prosperity. For twenty years I have been driving through South-East London to reach a house in Kent. My route takes me through a classic section of Cockney London, from the Shakespearean streets of Blackfriars and Southwark to Browning's Camberwell and Ruskin's Dulwich. During those twenty years I have watched the children growing pinker in cheek, their mothers smarter in dress, their fathers exchanging a motor bike for a family car. The houses are fresher painted, the laburnums and Japanese cherries blaze more profusely, the goods in the shopwindows approximate more and more closely to those of Piccadilly. Behind the façades I suspect that life is far gayer than it used to be. Old taboos are breaking down; the leaden respectability of a generation ago is softening under the influence of newer and brighter ideas.

Television has brought public figures, experimental theater, debatable topics, great events, into private lives. Everybody travels abroad, everybody reads. In a world where almost everybody leads a middle-class life—without, that is, extreme differences of income or privilege—snobberies get blurred. A tiny minority at the top can still keep aloof from the modern world for a few years more; a tiny minority at the bottom still suffer the rigors of inescapable poverty. But the immense majority consciously have a feeling of space and ease round them which their parents never knew. Probably they are unimaginative folk, not easily roused by anxieties and privations which they have not experienced in their own lives. Shifts in world power affect them much less than a rise in the bank rate; the disappearance of an empire passes almost unnoticed. I do not suppose that at any period a kind of calm happiness has been more widespread than it is in England today: not a heroic frame of mind, certainly, but a pleasant and comfortable one to live with.

Underneath the surface there are all kinds of tensions, naturally; and some of these Mr. Davidson has caught most cunningly. English civilization today is not only a middle-class but also a middle-aged experience. The old are likely to feel neglected and the young misunderstood. They are extremely serious, the young. They march against the atom bomb, they observe their elders with tense disapproval. A new Puritanism is on the way, with corresponding outbreaks of restlessness. Either the young purse their lips at the spectacle of parents dancing (or so it seems) while Rome is burning, or they dress up in tight pants and Italian shoes in order to be rude to Jamaicans on the street. The clever ones who have been to a university at public expense may have outsoared their own homes. They have shifted out of one social category without finding a place for themselves, as by right, in another: hence the sporadic appearance of Angry Young Men. And one and all are likely to feel that, although society owes them a debt, they have no corresponding debt to repay to society. Somebody somewhere will pay: Why should they?

This makes for political tranquillity, but also for apathy. After listening to talk in a French café or on an Italian market place, the English seem almost unbelievably acquiescent. Just because they have no Alabama, no Algeria, no Berlin, no Léopoldville right on their doorstep, they pretend that such places do not exist. I have the feeling that this riled Mr. Davidson. It has often riled me. There are moments in any experience of the English at home when one feels oneself to be drifting down an amiable backwater just when the thunder of Niagara is expected in vain. The Dickensian fog is momently closing in. But only momently. I believe Mr. Davidson would agree with my own verdict on my countrymen. Jogtrot they may be, and perhaps slightly dazed by their shifting international situation. But they still maintain the further Dickensian trait of allowing cheerfulness to keep breaking in. And so long as it does so, their reserves of steady good humor will remain a rich pool for the rest of Europe to draw upon.

A traveler on the moors at Campbeltown, Argyll

Gallery
Promenade
SEASON TICKETS ONLY
Promenade 3 – at Door 11

3

Beatnik concert outside Albert Hall, London

One-man demonstration for Sir Oswald Mosley in Trafalgar Square

Scrubwoman at a London advertising agency

On the strand, Brighton

Lady bowlers at Brighton

Fishwives at Tarbert in Scotland

By a cemetery in Whitby, Yorkshire

Boys at school at Pitlochry, Scotland

The Duke of Argyll before his castle

In the midst of traffic—anywhere in England

Special license: refreshment stand at a cricket match, Hastings

Age-old tradition: the Public House

Twentieth-century innovation: a London coffee bar

A residential street in Whitby, Yorkshire

At the Throckmorton Street corner of the Stock Exchange, after closing

Rooms for Improvement

When is a salon more than a drawing room? When one

goes, as in Paris, to be diverted and comes away instructed

"What became of that man I used to see sitting at the end of your table?" somebody asked the famous eighteenth-century Paris hostess, Mme Geoffrin.

"He was my husband. He is dead." It is the epitaph of all such husbands. The hostess of a salon (the useful word *salonnière*, unfortunately, is an Anglo-Saxon invention) must not be encumbered by family life, and her husband, if he exists, must know his place.

The salon was invented by the Marquise de Rambouillet at the beginning of the seventeenth century. She was half Italian, born in 1588 in Rome where her father was the French Ambassador. (It is worth noting that the French word *salon* derives from the Italian *salone*.) At the age of twelve she married the Marquis de Rambouillet, who provided her with a name, a house, and an income and, but for her, would never have been heard of.

Mme de Rambouillet began at the beginning: she designed and built a house in Paris suitable for the form of gathering she was to inaugurate. The Hôtel de Rambouillet stood on the present site of the Magasin du Louvre in the Rue de Rivoli. It was a complete departure from the existing type of nobleman's residence, where the reception rooms, painted dark brown or red, were so pompous, huge, and dreary that it had become the fashion for women to receive in their bedrooms, since these were the only intimate places in the house. Mme de Rambouillet designed a series of small sitting rooms leading out of each other and giving onto a beautiful garden filled, in summer, with orange and oleander trees; the rooms were cosy; they inspired confidences and long leisurely hours of talk. The blue room, hung with blue and white brocade on a gold ground, was her masterpiece and is famous in the history of house decoration.

When Mme de Rambouillet's house was ready, she filled it with people chosen because they could talk amusingly—another innovation. Instead of inviting only noblemen, she steered clear of court circles and surrounded herself with clever men: writers and artists of middle-class origin. Her literary star, Voiture, was the son of a wine merchant.

Mme de Rambouillet was not herself well educated (this applies to many of the women who have had salons), but she was attractive, had a talent for leading conversation, and made her house so gay and amusing that everybody longed to be invited there. Though she insisted on great politeness, she was a seventeenth- and not an eighteenth-century person, and like all her contemporaries she loved a practical joke. Once when Voiture wrote her a sonnet, she had it printed and sewn into an old anthology of verse which she then lent to the poet. When he came upon his poem he supposed it must be something he had once read, subconsciously remembered, and rewritten as his own. He was positively haunted by the affair until at last Mme de Rambouillet confessed all. To pay her back he got hold of two dancing bears which he brought into the blue room while she was reading poetry aloud. She suddenly perceived the addition to her audience reflected in a looking glass—we can imagine the result, screams of terror followed by screams of rage and then by screams of laughter.

Society in those days had its childish side. But if the tone at the Hôtel de Rambouillet was high-spirited, it was also serious. Not only was the company fond of intellectual parlor games—Voiture had a talent for setting rhymed conundrums—but the French language was under constant discussion. (The French Academy, whose function it is to preserve the language, was established in 1635.) Some contemporaries, jealous perhaps, were critical of the Rambouillet set. But the French aristocracy of that day had few interests beyond hunting and warfare and cared little for the things of the mind; the fact is that French conversation was first brought to a fine art at the Hôtel de Rambouillet. European civilization owes a debt to this Marquise.

Mme de Rambouillet's successors have been legion. The most famous of her immediate ones was Mlle de Scudéry

By NANCY MITFORD

In the fashionable salon of the Prince de Conti, guests take tea à l'anglaise *while the ten-year-old Mozart plays the harpsichord*

(1607–1701), herself a member of the Rambouillet set. She was a very clever person, well educated in every sense of the word. She spoke Spanish and Italian, painted, danced, wrote best-selling novels, and at the same time knew all about farming and gardening; she could cook and sew, make scents and preserves, and was an excellent sick-nurse. She was ugly even in her youth, and virtuous until her dying day (at ninety-four). She liked men better than women, however, and used to say that when women are together there is no interesting conversation: it always comes back to ribbons, gossip, or servants. The moment a man appears the tone changes. When men are together the talk may lack gaiety and lightness, but it is never dull—in short, we need them more than they need us. For conversation to be perfect, she felt, it should touch on many different subjects, never resting heavily on one; there must be no bitterness or disagreeable teasing, and it must never be improper. *"Esprit de politesse, esprit de joie."* Mlle de Scudéry entertained every Saturday; her guests included Mlle de Montpensier,

la Grande Mademoiselle, as well as Mme de Sévigné and Huet, one of the most learned men of the age.

Then there was the Marquise de Sablé (1599–1678), another hostess who moved in the same circles as Mlle de Scudéry. The bright particular star of *her* salon was the Duc de La Rochefoucauld, her lover. In 1662 Mme de Sablé abandoned the world, made a general confession, and entered a convent. Her guests and her Duke were taken over by the Comtesse de La Fayette (1634–1693). Nobody ever knew whether Mme de La Fayette and La Rochefoucauld were lovers, but he visited her every day until his death, and, as their mutual friend Bussy-Rabutin remarked, in such cases there is always love. Mme de La Fayette's husband lived in the country, so he did not interfere with this relationship whatever it may have been, but her little dog was furiously jealous of the Duke. To this day ghostly barks are heard in the old house in the Rue de Vaugirard at the very hour when he used regularly to pay his call.

Other members of Mme de La Fayette's salon included her

33

lifelong friend, the famous and delightful Marquise de Sévigné, Huet, Segrais the poet, Mignard the painter, the Marquise de Thianges (sister of Mme de Montespan, Louis XIV's mistress), and a flighty young couple, the Marquis and Marquise de Coulanges. Mme de Coulanges's confessor used to say: "This lady's sins are a series of epigrams." The great middle-class writers of the day, such as Racine, Molière, Pascal, and Boileau, do not seem ever to have been invited to the Rue de Vaugirard; La Fontaine went there once, but his manners were supposed to have been uncouth and he was not a success. Two great works of art, however, were the direct result of Mme de La Fayette's gatherings: her own novel, *La Princesse de Clèves*, and La Rochefoucauld's *Maximes*. Both these wonderful books were submitted at all stages to members of the salon to be polished and repolished; the historical details for *La Princesse de Clèves*, which is set in the court of Henry II, were lovingly studied; everybody was immersed in all the histories and memoirs that could be found.

Unlike Mme de Rambouillet, Mme de La Fayette was fond of high society and would really have liked a place at the court, which was now at Versailles; unfortunately, her two greatest friends, La Rochefoucauld and Cardinal de Retz, were looked on with no good eye by Louis XIV, since they had both taken part in the rebellion of the Fronde. Mme de Thianges knew that Mme de La Fayette longed to be received by the King; so she had a model made of her friend's salon with wax figures of all the habitués and presented this charming toy, which she called *La Chambre du Sublime*, to her nephew the Duc du Maine, in front of Louis XIV and the whole court. The King was intrigued and amused; he invited Mme de La Fayette to Versailles and himself showed her all the sights. If death had come upon her at that moment, she would have died happy.

Mlle de Scudéry

The eighteenth century differed from the seventeenth in manners, customs, and thought. People became more refined in their habits (cleaner for one thing), the minor arts were cultivated as never before or since, and the art of conversation rose to its zenith. A salon which could be said to bridge these two epochs was that of Mme de Lambert (1647–1733). For twenty years she was happily married to a rich banker; when he died she set up house in a wing of the Palais Mazarin (now the Bibliothèque Nationale) where she received society people and writers. It was said that she gave the *ton* (that untranslatable word) to a new era. Like many good hostesses she had a governessy side to her character: hers was the only house in Paris where no gambling was allowed; she frowned, too, on improper talk, which, she said, was the sign of a deranged heart and was not the least bit clever. Religion, even if one did not quite believe in it, was a decent sentiment much to be encouraged. She advised

her son to have mistresses superior to himself so that he would be kept up to the mark. "With one's equals one is apt to relax (*l'esprit s'assoupit*)." "Be kind to your servants," she said, "they are your unlucky friends." She laid down two excellent rules for conversation: no anecdotes, and never tell the same thing twice—not only not to the same people, but never at all. Talk should pour out quite fresh; once something has been said, the dew is off it.

The most famous of eighteenth-century salons—perhaps, indeed, of all French salons—was that of the Marquise du Deffand. Her long life (1697–1780) lasted from a year after the death of Mme de Sévigné to nine years before the French Revolution, and during all that time she hardly left Paris. She was beautiful, highly intelligent, and very funny. As a child she received almost no education; afterward, as autodidacts usually do, she cursed her parents for this, saying that she would not care to be young again unless she could be sure of having a worldly, clever man as tutor. She was engaged in a perpetual fight against boredom—the only enemy she ever feared. The trouble was that she could not believe that anything really mattered. A practicing Roman Catholic, she wished with all her heart to have faith; it seemed impolite to doubt, and, like Mme de Lambert, she regarded religion as a decent sentiment. But faith eluded her. For most of her life she had the same attitude toward love. Her husband bored her and she soon managed to get rid of him; thereafter she practiced love without believing in it, because it was the usual thing to do in her world.

She had love affairs with the Regent and others who moved in the same set; then she settled down, apparently for life, with Charles Hénault, Président of the *parlement* of Paris and great friend of Voltaire's. Their affair lasted forty years but was always rather tepid. When the Président was old and failing and so absent-minded that half the time he did not know where he was, she made him talk about another woman he had loved, Mme de Castelmoron. "Was she amusing, Président?" "Yes, indeed, very amusing." "More so than Mme du Deffand?" "Oh, no, that would be saying too much." "But which did you love the most?" "Ha! I loved Mme de Castelmoron!"

Mme du Deffand thought this exceedingly funny and told everybody. She had another liaison, with Pont-de-Veyle. Somebody once heard her say to him, "Few attachments have lasted as long as ours—fifty years, I should think?" "More than fifty," replied the old man. "And all that time, not a cloud, not a cross word." "I always think how wonderful that is!" he said. "But perhaps it is because we have really been rather indifferent to each other?" "Very possibly," replied Pont-de-Veyle.

It was not until she was quite middle-aged that her salon became famous. She was never rich, so she had no great house in which to entertain, but lived in a convent in the Rue St. Dominique (now the Ministry of War). "Here," said Président Hénault, "she gathered together a brilliant company; all deferred to her, she had a noble, generous heart. How many distinguished people would agree with this." Indeed, her friends loved her even if she rather alarmed them. The charm of her salon lay in the mixture of the people to be found there: aristocrats, writers, politicians, *les philosophes,* as well as any foreigner of note who happened to be visiting Paris. She liked to be surrounded by clever people in their party clothes and on their best behavior, but she had no desire for intimacy. She used to say that supper was one of the four ends of man and that she had forgotten what the other three were. Her guests would begin to arrive at about six; supper was at half past nine. Mme du Deffand went to bed only when she could no longer induce anybody to sit up and talk with her. She lived for these evening hours of conversation and filled in the rest of the long day as best she could.

When Mme du Deffand was fifty-five a ghastly misfortune overtook her. She became blind. She accepted the affliction with the stoicism of her race and class: it is not considered polite in France to complain of the blows of fate. "I am blind, Madame," she wrote to her aunt, the Duchesse de Luynes. "People praise my courage, but what would I gain by despairing?" So little fuss did she make, in fact, that her guests hardly realized that her sight was going. With the horror of total blindness approaching, she decided to have a change of air and went to stay with her brother on the family estate in Burgundy. Here she found a Cinderella-like figure leading a miserable existence, half servant, half poor relation: Julie de Lespinasse, the illegitimate daughter of her brother. Mme du Deffand took a fancy to this lively girl of twenty, and when she went back to Paris Julie went with her. She acted as secretary and reader to her aunt and was an enormous asset to the salon; everybody loved her and many fell in love with her, notably the great d'Alembert, one of Mme du Deffand's most regular guests.

For ten years the two women lived harmoniously, until Mme du Deffand suddenly became aware that the most brilliant members of her circle were in the habit of arriving early and going for a gossip and a giggle to Julie's room before turning up in the salon. Of course, by then they had already told their good stories and fired off their jokes; the cream had been skimmed from the milk. Mme du Deffand's rage knew no bounds; Julie was sent packing. But she did not go far. Her friends soon found her a flat in the next street, the Rue de Bellechasse, and here she set up a rival establishment, soon to become as famous as that of her aunt. Parisians now had to choose between the two ladies because Mme du Deffand absolutely refused to receive anybody who

Mlle de Lespinasse

went to her niece. Julie took away the philosophic and progressive element in French society; her salon was more intellectual and Mme du Deffand's more fashionable and political.

So strange is fate: both women are now famous for their love letters, which have become classics of the French language. That Julie, young, poor, and romantic, should have suffered from unrequited love was almost to be expected; that Mme du Deffand, at sixty-eight and stone blind, with her worldly wisdom and after the life she had led, should have caught the same complaint seems incredible. Yet so it was. The crotchety, cynical, spiteful, clever, fashionable, witty son of a great father, Horace Walpole, twenty years younger than she, became the object of this unnatural and celebrated passion. Mlle de Lespinasse's love affair followed a more usual pattern. Her lover was an uninteresting young man named Guibert. He played fast and loose with her, married someone else, and yet never quite broke off his relationship with Julie. So here were the aunt and the niece, living only a few yards from each other, both suffering the tortures of the damned, dividing between them all the amusing elements of French society. Mme du Deffand never forgave, and when, in 1776, Julie died of a broken heart, she wrote without emotion: "Mlle de Lespinasse died last night. Once this would have been an event in my life, but today it is nothing at all."

The eighteenth-century salons of which there were many, with Mme du Deffand's as the archetype—were temples dedicated to conversation. Only good talkers were admitted; the be-all and end-all of the evening was the cut and thrust of their encounters. If many of the guests were writers, that was because they had more to talk about than other people. Politicians as such were not sought after. One of Mme du Deffand's favorites, however, was the Duc de Choiseul, who governed France for twelve years; when he left his office desk behind him at Versailles, he had no desire to talk shop. Politics then were thought as dull as big business is now—in fact, were always referred to as business: *les affaires.* But as the century drew to its revolutionary close, *les affaires* began to affect people's lives and therefore to interest everybody, and the salons became more and more political until they were a hotbed of intrigues and plots.

After that the heavy atmosphere of the nineteenth century, with its messages and meanings, its reforms, its scientific discoveries and German philosophy, fell like a wet blanket on the world, extinguishing the flame of pure pleasure which had hitherto burned so brightly in France. I do not think we should have cared to have been bossed by Mme de Staël, to have plotted at Mme Roland's, or to have drunk tea and eaten biscuits, Thackeray and Mrs. Gaskell our fellow guests, at Mme Mohl's (born Mary Clarke);

while heaven preserve us from such Sunday evenings as those of Marie d'Agoult, which she described as "a burgeoning of youth." The only nineteenth-century salon to compare for brilliant amusement with that of Mme du Deffand was presided over by Princesse Mathilde (1820–1904).

Mathilde Bonaparte was the daughter of Napoleon's youngest brother, Jérôme, and Princess Catherine of Württemberg, through whom she was closely related to the Czar of Russia and Queen Victoria. She took no account, however, of these royal relations, regarding herself as a Bonaparte, a Corsican; she positively worshiped the memory of Napoleon. "The French Revolution," she used to say, "why, if it had never happened I should be selling oranges in the streets of Ajaccio! I am not one of those Princesses by divine right." Like Mme de Rambouillet she was brought up in Rome; after an early engagement to her cousin Louis Napoleon, which came to nothing, she was married off by her impecunious father to the richest man in Europe, Prince Demidov, who owned the Ural mines. He is always supposed to have been quite impossible and to have treated her like a brute, but in fact he had just cause for complaint. In St. Petersburg his family were regarded as vulgar parvenus; when the newly married couple arrived at the great Demidov palace, Princesse Mathilde was invited to the Court and to various aristocratic houses without her husband, a state of affairs to which she raised no objection. In any case her only desire was to get to Paris. Nothing pleased her in Russia, where court life was too stiff and too dowdy, while the gypsies whom her husband frequented were dirty and dull. It was not easy to leave Russia, even in those days, and in spite of her friendship with her cousin the Czar, she was obliged to bribe her way out with jewels. *"Paris vaut bien des émeraudes,"* she said. Her marriage soon came to an end, but the Czar saw to it that she had a huge settlement.

She set up house in the Rue de Courcelles, where she was surrounded by the most interesting men of the day. In spite of her name she never played at politics. When she first lived in Paris, Louis Philippe was on the throne. She was fond of him and his family, and, like Louis Napoleon's half brother, the Duc de Morny, she was sorry when they were chased into exile. However, like the Duc de Morny, she had a favored place under the Second Empire, which soon consoled her; indeed, until Louis Napoleon married, she acted as hostess for him. Understandably there was no love lost between her and Eugénie, and after the marriage Princesse Mathilde retired from the Court. Soon she was receiving on a large scale at the Rue de Courcelles.

She dined every evening at seven-thirty with a few intimates; after dinner she was at home to the members of her circle. Her lover was Count Nieuwerkerke, director of the Louvre—a Don Juan, a dandy, and a rake, who treated her abominably and whom her other guests cordially disliked. He was always there, however, deferred to in everything. In 1860 she struck up a friendship with Sainte-Beuve, and her salon, which had hitherto been composed of society people, generals, politicians, and museum officials, became almost entirely literary. The Goncourt brothers, Taine, Renan, Mérimée, Dumas, Victor Hugo, Thiers, and in later years the young Proust and Hérédia were all regular guests. Flaubert read his *Education sentimentale* aloud to her; she was one of the first to appreciate his genius. Gautier sat cross-legged at her feet like a Turk, until the horror of the modern world became too much for him and he died of melancholy in 1872. Certain writers, however, could not get on with her. Daudet went twice to the Rue de Courcelles, said the food was bad, and never returned. Musset went but arrived an hour late, blind drunk, and was not asked again. George Sand went only once and never spoke the whole evening. Mathilde, on the whole, did not like women: "If a woman comes into the room I have to change the conversation."

The house in the Rue de Courcelles, which still exists and is much used now for charity bazaars, was typical of the nineteenth century—huge and gloomy, with great drawing rooms of bad proportions leading out of each other. Princesse Mathilde blanketed the walls with velvet draperies and covered them with second-rate pictures. Her conservatory was said to be like several junk shops in a virgin forest; even her contemporaries thought it awful. She herself was very much of her generation, though her natural and direct manner of speech sometimes startled the famous men around her. She had a strong—we should think exaggerated—family feeling, as people had in those days. Nobody was allowed to breathe a word against the Bonapartes. She quarreled with Sainte-Beuve because he joined a newspaper where they were spoken of, she thought, unsuitably, and she argued with Sardou over his *Madame Sans-Gêne.* Taine sent her his *Origines de la France contemporaine,* in which there is some mild criticism of Napoleon; she ordered her carriage and left a card at his house with "P.P.C." on it (*pour prendre congé,* the French way of saying good-bye).

Just before the Second Empire fell, Nieuwerkerke, feeling that Mathilde could be of no more use to him, left her. He had been so horrid to her for so long that his departure was more of a relief than a sorrow. She moved to a smaller house in the Rue de Berri, taking a young female companion to live there with her. A new lover appeared on the scene; the salon was more brilliant than ever and its hostess was considered to be one of the glories of the Third Republic. Alas, the companion made off with the lover. Although Princesse Mathilde was nearly seventy when she discovered their liaison, her Corsican temperament was as violent as ever and she was terribly unhappy. In spite of faithful friends who did everything they could think of to console her, her last years were darkened by this affair. She died in 1904.

One of the best-known French salons in the early years of the twentieth century existed, strange to say, in Berlin. It was that of Princess Radziwill, a Frenchwoman descended from Talleyrand. She entertained a cosmopolitan society,

Amid potted palms and nineteenth-century clutter, Princesse Mathilde Bonaparte (in white) presides over her salon in the Rue de Courcelles

but no word of German was allowed in her drawing room and indeed once, dining with the Kaiser, she sat arms folded, not eating a mouthful, because the menu was in German. When she lay on her deathbed during the war of 1914, she was asked what she would like. "A French priest and one of my children" was the answer. Her house, the great Radzi-will palace, then became the Chancellery, and Hitler met his end in its cellars.

In Paris Mme de Caillavet, the friend of Anatole France, exercised a powerful influence with members of the Academy. Between the two wars the American Miss Natalie Barney (who is still, happily, with us and still lives in the same lovely old house) entertained a brilliant Franco-American society in the Rue Jacob.

When I first lived in Paris in 1945, there were several salons which were amusing to visit, but the only one with a truly cosy and intimate character was that of the Comtesse Marie-Blanche de Polignac. She entertained musicians; the musical scene in Paris has not been the same since her death several years ago.

The great days of the salon seem to be over for the present. Society is too diffuse; people are too busy; manners have become too casual. (In the old days if a hostess wished to indicate that somebody should not come back without a definite invitation, she would herself conduct him to the door. The intimates came and went without ceremony. A modern hostess would find that few of her guests would take such a delicate hint.) Where there used to be one or two foreign visitors to Paris, there are now a million. Even the French travel more than formerly. The essence of a salon is that its members are constantly together; they know each other so well that nothing has to be explained—they talk almost in a form of shorthand. With half the company away putting on plays in South America, lecturing in Athens, attending P.E.N. club meetings in Brussels, and so on, their intimacy would constantly be interrupted.

But perhaps when the atom bomb has cleared the air and when atomic energy has given back leisure to the world, there will once more be small gatherings of Frenchmen, looking like Hindu gods or Picasso paintings because of the fall-out, but none the less clever for that, ready to sit up all night with some brilliant and sympathetic hostess, enjoying the pleasures of repartee.

Nancy Mitford is equally at home in the eighteenth century (her biographies of Voltaire and Mme de Pompadour) and the twentieth (her sparkling novels, of which the most recent is Don't Tell Alfred), *but has little use for the nineteenth.*

Though it is the function of creative writers to concern themselves with the condition of man, it is not often that one of them plunges far into the specific field of the science of man. Yet Robert Ardrey, playwright (Thunder Rock; Shadow of Heroes), novelist (Brotherhood of Fear), and author of some outstanding American screenplays, has ever since youth been a student of anthropology. Recent trips of his to Africa, to observe at first hand the startling finds of primate remains and to talk with their finders, have led him to expand on the revolutionary theory that man may be the direct descendant of a species of flesh-eating, predatory apes whose special genius consisted in discovering and applying what was to become man's most distinctive and prized possession: the weapon.

Ardrey's belief, supported by some anthropologists, is that man's immediate forbear was a creature known as Australopithecus africanus. This animal had man's erect carriage, his feet and dental structure; most strikingly, he had lost the prominent canine teeth of other primates and must have relied on some other means of self-protection. What could this have been? The clues, Ardrey believes, are the animal bones found along with those of Australopithecus. These include animal skulls bashed in by a double-headed object—and antelope thighbones with a double end that just fits the holes in the skulls. The evidence suggests Australopithecus, though not yet a man, used this blunt instrument to kill.

Any such theory of man's origin must be regarded as speculative. But Ardrey's conclusion, from the evidence already in, is that man's very humanness lies in his use of weapons, that the instinct for violence is written into his genes. He meditates on man's nature ("How would you have survived, O Adam, without fangs or claws, without pointed horns or leather hide, or a snout to sniff with or feet to climb with. . . . How could you have survived, O most vulnerable primate, tuskless in Paradise, had you not been created with a weapon in your hand?") and goes on to speculations about the coming destiny of earth's great weapon-bearer. From the ironic yet poetic text of his reflections (to be issued this month under the title African Genesis by Atheneum Publishers) HORIZON has chosen the excerpt that follows.

HOW CAN MAN GET ALONG WITHOUT WAR?

In some remote past he was born with a weapon in his hand. Long evolution has made over his body but never tamed his predatory nature. Now, says an eloquent student of anthropology, his only chance to escape a nuclear doom is to conquer the deepest instinct of his species

If you will go to the bathroom, lock the door, and observe yourself closely with neither shame nor pretension, you will discover yourself in the presence of a mammal so primitive and so generalized as to be difficult to describe. You have no distinctive horns arranged like a musical instrument on top of your head. Nobody would dream of shooting you for your tusks. Your hide is worthless, your vestigial fur of comic proportions. No intricate patterns adorn your surface; it has neither the camouflage value to make possible your vanishing into a landscape, nor such decorative value as to warrant your being nailed to a wall. Your teeth lack any special superiority, either for munching hay, chiseling through doors, or penetrating jugular veins. Your claws are so inadequate that while a kitten may scratch you, you cannot scratch the kitten back. And while it is true that you are warm-blooded, that you do not lay eggs, and that you are edible, still the same things may be said of all mammals.

Evolution is largely a story of advancing specialization. Time, change, and natural selection combine to create natural values particularly adapted to special spheres of existence. From the point of view of evolution, therefore, it is the specialized animal that must be regarded as the more advanced; the animal retaining his generality, the more primitive. Man, for instance, is on the whole a more primitive creature anatomically than the gorilla.

The Species with Outsized Buttocks

It is not, of course, that you have entirely failed to acquire specializations. You have a moderately outsized head, and thoroughly outsized buttocks. Also, you have flat feet, a chin, and an embarrassing lack of fur. But a zoologist visiting from some distant planet, having overcome his first

By ROBERT ARDREY

repugnance for a mammal almost as hairless as a hippopotamus, will probably not be unduly fascinated by your head size. Enlargement of the brain is a primate, not just human, characteristic. What will enthrall him will be the magnificent development of the human buttocks and the peculiar specialization of feet.

Nowhere in a world of marmosets and macaques, of gibbons and mountain gorillas, of lemurs and howling monkeys and chacma baboons will you find anything to compare with the feet and buttocks that you are now observing behind locked doors. Regard them with pride. They may be afflicted with broken arches and a bad sacroiliac. That is only because these marks of your kind have been recently acquired and could do with another mutation or two. But even as they will fascinate the visiting zoologist, your feet and your buttocks should fascinate you. They are the changes favored by nature to promote your firm concord with terrestrial existence.

The specialized human foot makes possible a balanced, erect posture and rapid movement without recourse to an all-fours position. No ape or monkey has the capacity. He may stand erect momentarily, or stagger along for a distance, but his hands are never freed permanently for chores other than locomotion. Similarly, the special development of that mass of muscle centered in the human buttocks makes possible agility and all the turning and twisting and throwing and balance of the human body in an erect position. As the brain co-ordinates our nervous activity, so the buttocks co-ordinate our muscular activity. No ape boasts such a muscular monument to compare with ours; and it is a failure more fundamental than his lack of an enlarged brain.

There is one last distinction that came your way, and I have almost forgotten it. Peer into the bathroom mirror once more and observe that bony projection known as a chin. Feel it with awe. Apes had a little bony brace on the inside angle of the V of their lower jaw to tie the halves of the jawbone together. The human stock from *Proconsul* down through Neanderthal man could do no better than to thicken the bone for strength. Then came your particular species in the human family, *Homo sapiens*. And at the last evolutionary moment chance presented your jaw with a flying buttress to reinforce the V.

By this single distinction, the chin, will paleontologists of far distant times, sorting through the fossils, be enabled to classify our kind from all other primate kinds, human and prehuman, that have gone before us. There is no other final distinction. Shave it with respect.

Man is a zoological group of sentient rather than sapient beings, characterized by a brain so large that he uses rather little of it, a chin distinctive enough to identify him among related animals, and an overpowering enthusiasm for things that go *boom*. Aside from these attributes—and the chin merely distinguishes *Homo sapiens* from earlier members of the human family—it is difficult to say where man began

and the animal left off. We have a quality of self-awareness uncommon among animals, but whether this is a consequence of the enlarged brain or was shared with our extinct fathers we do not know.

In any event we do have the power to be aware of self and to visualize ourselves in a present or future situation. And the power dictates as entirely natural our curiosity concerning the human outcome. Whether self-awareness will actually influence that outcome must strike any observer of human behavior, on the basis of past performance, as dubious. When human consciousness of potential disaster has in the past come into conflict with instincts of animal origin, our record has been one of impeccable poverty. No past situation, however, can compare with the contemporary predicament of potential nuclear catastrophe. And self-awareness, generating mortal fear, may at least partially forestall an evolutionary disaster.

Obeying the Weapons Instinct

I find it convenient to consider the contemporary predicament in terms of three possible outcomes of varying probability, and the reader must forgive me if I do not seem to take the first two seriously. There is the first possibility—which I regard as remote—that *Homo sapiens* will obey his weapons instinct with minimum inhibition, put to full use his intellectual resources, and commit himself and his planet to a maximum explosion. The experiment of the enlarged brain, by its final action, will have been demonstrated a total failure. Allied to the carnivorous way, reason in one fiery instant will have demonstrated its inadequacy as a guiding force for living beings.

To believe that man has the capacity, however, even through a maximum effort, to bring an end to all life on our planet is a melodramatic expression of our treasured notion of man as the center of the universe. We have no such power. The ancient insect has mutational receptivity equal to our best efforts. While a giant effort on the part of man could conceivably bring extinction to all land vertebrates, it is impossible to believe that a world of insects would not survive. We may regret the passing of the lion, of the elephant, of our partners the horse and the sparkling dog. But natural selection, regretting nothing, will turn its attention to the instinctual promise of the termite, the ant, and the subtle bee.

I find that I have small patience with this first outcome —purple in its hues, pat in its outline—which has so entranced our neo-romantics. And so I leave it to consider the far higher probability of the second. This second field of probabilities grants, like the first, that man, sooner or later, will obey his weapons instinct. Given access to our traditional materials, we shall proceed with alacrity to blow up the place. It presumes, however, that we will fail to do quite such a job of it. The instinct to preserve the species runs deep in all animals, and it may compromise the effectiveness of our weapons compulsion. Or the enlarged brain may not succeed in perfecting a cataclysm of such devastating proportions. Whatever the ingredients of the partial disaster—whether instinctual, ineffectual, accidental, or even thoughtful—the second possible outcome presumes that a portion of mankind survives.

If I were a fox, or a reedbuck, or a rabbit, and I found myself among perhaps 20 per cent of my kind to survive a holocaust, I should face the future with equanimity. In a few generations select territories, abundant food supply, and compensatory breeding would restore my kind to its former fullness. But I am neither fox, nor reedbuck, nor rabbit. I am a human being dependent on society and technology. And were I to find myself among the 20 per cent of human beings to survive a contest of radiant weapons, I should much prefer to have been numbered among the victims.

One may, of course, take a hopeful view of such a colossal weeding of the human garden. Five hundred million people remain, but overpopulation will cease to be a problem in India, and traffic jams in New York. The Riviera will no longer be crowded in August, and there will be seats on commuter trains in the six o'clock rush.

Yet the survivor will face plague unrivaled in the Middle Ages and famine unknown in China's worst seasons. Social anarchy will grip him. The peasant will be murdered by marauding bands, the city man withered by his dependence on society. Disease, hunger, predation, and suicide will decimate the five hundred million, and mutation will alter the remainder's descendants.

Yet a certain strange hope exists. Any radiant catastrophe killing a presumed four-fifths of the human population will induce mutations in the majority of the survivors. Ninety-nine out of every one hundred mutations will be unfavorable. One will be benevolent. And here, should the second outcome provide mankind with its fate, lies evolution's hope.

The Day of Another Race

It is the paradox of the contemporary predicament that the force we have fashioned and that can destroy our species is the same force that can produce another.

Let us assume that among the 500 million immediate survivors of a nuclear contest, 100 million survive the post-apocalypse. Of the 100 million, perhaps half will have descendants suffering mutations. 49,500,000 will be doomed. But a half million will have descendants with endowments superior to the ancestral line. And it is on the shoulders of this slim half million that primate hopes must rest.

A grand and tragic breed will have passed from the earth; and the engine of our creation will have proved the engine of our destruction. But we shall leave behind no barren tidings. Here and there, in unlikely valleys and on unlikely plains, a few mutant beings will roam the byways as others once haunted the Lake Victoria shore. And natural selection will find them, these superior creatures: a few here, in a moss-draped swamp of the Mississippi delta; a few there, in a windy Himalayan pass; a handful, wandering the green velvet of an Argentine grassland; a solitary figure on an old Greek island, pausing in wonder before a marble memory. Slowly, ever so slowly, the mutant beings of a fiery creation will assemble their genetic promises, and a new species will be born. Is it too much to hope that in such a species reason will perhaps be an instinct?

The first outcome of the modern predicament must leave evolution to the neo-romantics. The second, more probable and more horrid in outline, at least allows man his evolutionary dignity. Yet there is a possible third outcome, in which very little happens at all.

The third possible outcome of the modern predicament assumes that we have already seen or shall shortly see the end of general warfare. Either a contest of ultimate weapons will never take place; or if it does take place, the contest will be of small biological significance in which no more than two or three hundred million people are killed. In either case, sufficient inhibition will have been created to hold in check the weapons instinct. And I regard this outcome as the most frightening if for no other reason than that it is the only one that a nearly intact humanity would have to live with.

How can we get along without war? It is the supreme question for our times. For war has been the most natural mode of human expression since the beginnings of recorded history, and the improvement of the weapon has been man's principal preoccupation since Bed Two in the Olduvai Gorge. What will happen to a species denied in the future its principal means of expression and its only means, in last appeal, of resolving differences?

Let us not be too hasty in our dismissal of war as an unblemished evil. Are you a Christian? Then recall that Christendom survived its darkest hour in the fury of the Battle of Tours. Do you believe in law? The rule of law became a human institution in the shelter of the Roman legions. Do you subscribe to the value of individual worth? Only by the success of the phalanx at Marathon did the Greeks repel the Persian horde and make possible the Golden Age.

No man can regard the way of war as good. It has simply been our way. No man can evaluate the eternal contest of weapons as anything but the sheerest waste and the sheerest folly. It has been simply our only means of final arbitration.

The true predicament of contemporary man is not entirely unlike the Pliocene predicament of the gorilla. The bough was the focus of his experience, as the weapon has been the focus of ours. It provided him with the fruit that was his nourishment and with his means of locomotion. It dominated his existence even to the specialization of his anatomy; his hooklike thumbs, his powerful chest, his long arms, his weak and truncated legs. The bough was the focus of gorilla tradition, gorilla instinct, gorilla security, gorilla psyche, and of the only way of life the gorilla knew. Then a natural challenge—the twelve million years of the drought-stricken Pliocene era deprived him of his bough. And the gorilla took to the ground. There we find him today, a depleted crew of evolutionary stragglers. Every night he builds a nest in tribute to ancestral memories. Every day he pursues the unequal struggle with extinction. His vitality sags. He defends no territory, copulates rarely. And the story of the gorilla will end, one day, not with a bang but a whimper.

Back to the Canebrakes?

Deprived of the contest of weapons that was the only bough he knew, it would seem that man must descend to the canebrakes of a new mode of existence. There he must find new dreams, new dynamics, new experiences to absorb him, new means of resolving his issues and of protecting whatever he regards as good. And he will find them; or he will find himself lost. Slowly his governments will lose their force and his societies their integration. Moral order, sheltered throughout all history by the judgment of arms, will fall away in rot and erosion. Insoluble quarrels will rend peoples once united by territorial purpose. Insoluble conflicts will split nations once allied by a common dream. Anarchy, ultimate enemy of social man, will spread its gray, cancerous tissues through the social corpus of our kind. Bandit nations will hold the human will a hostage, in perfect confidence that no superior force can protect the victim. Bandit gangs will have their way along the social thoroughfare, in perfect confidence that the declining order will find no means to protect itself. Every night we shall build our nostalgic family nest in tribute to ancestral memories. Every day we shall pursue through the fearful canebrakes our unequal struggle with extinction.

How can man get along without his wars and his weapons? Have we within our human resource the capacity to discover new dreams, new dynamisms? Or are we so burdened by our illusions and our pathetic rationalizations of the human condition that we can acknowledge no destiny beneath the human star but to go blindly blundering into a jingo jungle toward an indeterminate, inglorious, inexorable end?

It is an unpromising portrait. The miracle of man, however, is not how far he has sunk but how magnificently he has risen. No creature who began as a mathematical improbability, who was selected through millions of years of unprecedented environmental hardship and change for ruggedness, ruthlessness, cunning, and adaptability, and who in the short ten thousand years of what we may call civilization has achieved such wonders as we find about us, may be regarded as a creature without promise.

It is my belief that civilization is a normal evolutionary development in our kind, and a product of natural selection. So far as we know, it lacks direct animal origin. Like the jackdaw flock, our civilization is the bearer of social wisdom and the accumulated experience of our kind; but unlike the flock it carries no instinctual authority over the conduct of its members. Nevertheless, I believe that civilization has

come to mankind as neither accident nor ornament. It reflects the command of the kind. It rests on the most ancient of animal laws, that commanding order, and acts as a necessary inhibition and sublimation of predatory energies that would otherwise long ago have destroyed our species. I regard it as anything but a coincidence that the rate of civilization's rise has corresponded so closely with man's ascendant capacity to kill.

Civilization is a compensatory consequence of our killing imperative; the one could not exist without the other. It is at best a jerry-built structure, and a more unattractive edifice could scarcely be imagined. Its grayness is appalling. Its walls are cracked and eggshell thin. Its foundations are shallow, its antiquity slight. No bands boom, no flags fly, no glamourous symbols invoke our nostalgic hearts. Yet however humiliating the path may be, man beset by anarchy, banditry, chaos, and extinction must in last resort turn to that chamber of dull horrors, human enlightenment. For he has nowhere else to turn.

If man is to survive without war, a gloomier conclusion could not be written than that this structure must become our court of last appeal. It has failed us consistently in the past. It tends to fall down every thousand years or so. If the corridors of human enlightenment are to provide us with salvation, then a drearier whimper, one might almost conclude, could scarcely be imagined. Let us have the bang.

The Figure in the Back Room

But the choice is not ours. Never to be forgotten, to be neglected, to be derided, is the inconspicuous figure in the quiet back room. He sits with head bent, silent, waiting, listening to the commotion in the streets. He is the keeper of the kinds.

Who is he? We do not know. Nor shall we ever. He is a presence, and that is all. But his presence is evident in the last reaches of infinite space beyond man's probing eye. His presence is asserted in all things that ever were, and in all things that will ever be. And as his command is unanswerable, his identity is unknowable. But his most ancient concern is with order.

You may sense his word in the second law of thermodynamics, or the patterned behavior of brook trout in a clear New Zealand pool. You may find his word in the forms of cities and symphonies, of Rembrandts and fir trees and cumulus clouds.

Where a child is born, or a man lies dead; where life must go on, though tragedy deny it; where a farmer replants fields again, despoiled by flood or drought; where men rebuild cities that other men destroy; where tides must ebb as tides have flowed; there, see his footprints.

He does not care about you, or about me, or about man, for that matter. He cares only for order. But whatever he says, we shall do. He is rising now, in civilization's quiet back room, and he is looking out the window.

PAVILIONS ON THE PRAIRIE

Bruce Goff, the Oklahoma architect, designs every house as if it were the first one in

PHOTOGRAPHS JOE D. PRICE

Bruce Goff designed this Oklahoma Shangri-La for a bachelor whose way of life didn't require the multiple rooms and facilities of the conventional family dwelling. As the floor plan below shows, it consists of a triangular studio-living room with projecting wings for carport, bedroom, and porch. The exterior combines massive walls of glistening anthracite and green glass cullets with sleek planes of gold anodized aluminum. Inside, thick white nylon carpeting covers the entire living area (above); it flows down the slanting walls (used as back rests), across the floor, and into the hexagonal "conversation pit." Guests remove their shoes before entering this luxurious room. An article on Goff's architecture, by John Canaday, begins on the next page.

1 carport and entrance
2 storage
3 photo storage and exhibition wall
4 conversation pit
5 bathroom
6 bedroom
7 kitchen
8 porch
9 pools

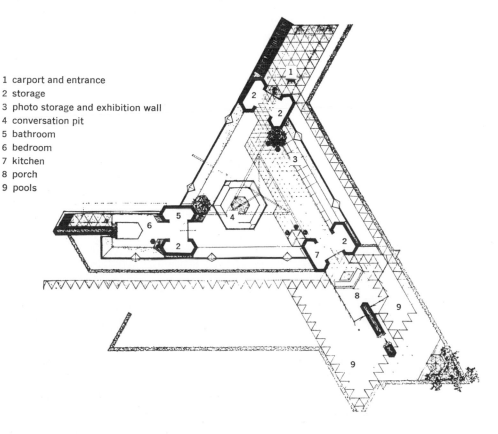

The shingled domes of this house in Illinois are built around standard Quonset ribs—an example of Goff's free, imaginative use of materials.

Some decades ago a revolutionary generation of architects rejected the traditional concept of the house as "a box with holes punched in it." They succeeded in establishing a replacement pattern, which is now familiar to everybody and is called to mind for most people by the word "modern." But with the battle won, a few restive spirits are wondering whether the crystallization of a modern style hasn't left us holding the same old architectural bag in the form of another kind of box with other kinds of holes punched in it.

The modern box-house may be of glass, or it may be of brick or concrete, and it may be a compound of several boxes staggered on stilts and admitting light through slits, bands, and other neo-hole apertures. But as long as it remains a box, Bruce Goff, for one, is throwing it out. Some of his exuberantly non-box structures illuminate these pages.

Goff is a fifty-seven-year-old architect working out of Bartlesville, Oklahoma, who might be called antimodern or supermodern, depending. He would be as unlikely to build you a twentieth-century "machine for living" as an eighteenth-century Georgian mansion, but he would probably prefer the Georgian mansion if forced to a choice. "Living" is the key to his concept of a house, but "machine" is antithetic to it.

Goff's houses deny the validity of standardization as a way of life and proclaim that each human being is an individual whose inner self is more important than the outer casing by which he meets his obligations as a social unit. A man's house is the place where the spirit unique to himself must be expressed and nourished; hence any standardized architectural casing, "modern" or other, should be unthinkable.

By architectural truism a good house accommodates the activities to be carried on in it, with proportionate recognition of space for cooking, eating, sleeping, and even the pursuit of hobbies. But the average architect seldom gets beyond the rumpus-room concept of the spiritual life. A Goff house is planned as if such a thing as a house had never existed before, as if an individual had suddenly originated the idea that it is possible to have a place of your own where the things you live by are given physical accommodation. This first house in the world would be like nothing ever seen before and so, usually, is a Goff house, in a world where houses have been seen by the millions.

Since his philosophy begins with the premise of individual spiritual values engaged in a battle for survival in a world dedicated to conformity, Goff is a romantic at heart. But he differs in a fundamental way from his nineteenth-century cousins who popularized a more obvious approach to romantic architectural design. Just before that century opened, an eccentric Englishman named William Beckford commissioned the architect James Wyatt to create for him a pseudo-Gothic abbey as a kind of domestic stage setting suited to romantic attitudinizing. Goff shares Beckford's idea that house architecture, to be any good, must be integrated with personal values, but instead of borrowing old forms already infused with romantic associations, he invents new ones. This is a whopping difference.

Such inventions need not be quixotic in conception to be wildly romantic in visual effect. By pure theory we can even argue that the more fantastic they appear, the more likely they are to be structural forms devised to accommodate the physical requirements of the kind of living peculiar to the inhabitant, and to accommodate them in a way harmonious with his reasons for living as he does. Goff attaches as much

In Gulfport, Mississippi, Goff raised this triangular house on stilts to take advantage of the view and to avoid flooding from the bayou.

This Florida house is a series of fourteen-foot cubes arranged so that the interior is spacious enough for parties yet intimate enough for two.

importance to practicality of plan and construction as do the most severe functionalists, but he does not hold to the same definition of what practicality is. He regards it as a variable that changes its nature in relation to situations and temperaments. The functionalist regards it as a constant, the same for everybody.

Thus the idea that "form follows function," a phrase turned into a bromide in the first half of our century to justify the harsh monotony or elegant antisepsis of a new academic style, is released from a strait jacket that makes it only half-operative as a doctrine. Instead of standardized elements in multiple recombinations, the freed doctrine produces original forms that appear only once because they satisfy functions, including intangible ones, unique to a single structure. In functional romanticism—and God forbid that the term should ever catch on—the romantic impulse is fulfilled rather than reduced by its subjection to material realization as structure. Form following function by way of individual perception becomes expression. The material, in a double sense, if you wish, becomes the spiritual. And since this is a definition of art, the architect becomes an artist.

Artistry of form is inseparable from artistry in the use of materials, with Frank Lloyd Wright's near-mystical response to field stone and natural wood at one end of the range, and at the other, the functional respect for the sleekness of steel, aluminum, plate glass, and the rest. But the vocabulary of materials like the vocabulary of form can become a habit, and Goff disapproves of this habit along with all others. He has built walls of such unexpected materials as chunks of anthracite coal combined with greenish cullet —the waste left over after the manufacture of glass—and he

has covered the center portion of a muted gold ceiling with white goose feathers.

Theory aside, or satisfied, there comes a point where any imaginative architect with a sympathetic client must extend even the most practical concept into the area of free invention and embellishment. It would be foolish to pretend that every element in the houses on these pages is the automatic result of a practical solution, unless we romanticize the term "function" to the point of meaninglessness. Goff is a maverick, an extremist of sorts, maybe an exuberant oddity; in any case he is certainly a very personal architect. He supplies the "farthest-out" answers to questions many architects are asking themselves and to which they are supplying less startling answers.

This means that Goff is part of a romantic impulse in architecture today, but it does not mean that there is a neo-romantic school, which implies an organized movement, or a neo-romantic style, which means a set of forms accepted for repetition and recombination. There will be a neo-romantic style when forms of individually invented structures like Goff's are repeated less to perform the functions they were invented to serve than for the air of fantasy they more or less incidentally create. This is the repetitious history of the development and deterioration of architectural styles— the vulgarization of integral innovations into superimposed clichés. The neo-non-box may yet join the neo-box as a familiar residential form, and in that case pseudo-Goff could join pseudo-Gothic as a stage setting instead of a fitting habitation.

John Canaday, art editor of the New York Times, *wrote "Gargoyles for the Machine Age" in* HORIZON, *March, 1961.*

1 entrance
2 revolving closet
3 visiting area
4 future fireplace (suspended)
5 pool
6 dining table
7 breakfast area
8 kitchen
9 central support pipe
10 mechanical equipment
11 stairs to bathroom
12 stairs to upper levels

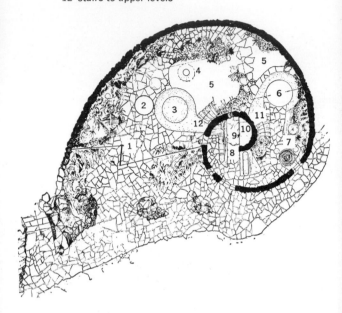

Goff's most arresting design is this spiral house in Norman, Oklahoma, which coils around a central steel pole from which the roof is suspended. It was planned for a family of four specifically to accommodate their own needs and interests, one of which is raising plants indoors. What Goff gave them was a continuous flow of space without partitions or rooms in the conventional sense. Shown opposite are the indoor pool, dining area, curving sandstone wall, and ribbonlike skylight which provides sunlight for the plants. The gold-carpeted saucer above the table is the children's play area, which projects out from the central core. Similar saucers, stepped up at intervals of three feet and reached by winding stairs, are used as living and sleeping areas. What this house lacks in privacy it makes up for in untrammeled space.

1 entrance
2 revolving closet
3 visiting area with Goff-designed lounge
4 parents' sleeping area
5 stairs to bathroom
6 dining table
7 play area
8 child's sleeping area
9 skylight
10 studio

46

Jules Feiffer's Wicked Eye and Ear

By RUSSELL LYNES

The satirist Jules Feiffer shares the common aversion to explosions, as he went to some pains to explain in one of his cartoon strips called "Boom!" He's something of an explosion himself. It took what seemed to him a long time for the fuse to burn down to the charge, but when it did, the bang it made was splendid. At first, its reverberations were heard mainly in a picturesque province of Greater New York known to its citizens as "the Village," for Feiffer's first cartoons appeared in *The Village Voice,* a provincial weekly. Up to that time he had been variously a boy who hated the high school he went to in the Bronx, a soldier who despised the Army, a struggling commercial artist who disliked working for other cartoonists and laying out throwaways. His childhood and young manhood, in other words, were normal. The noise that he finally made when he exploded, however, was abnormal.

It is difficult, indeed, to think of anyone in recent years who, speaking with such a quiet public voice, has made such a big noise. Since 1958, when his simply drawn and incisively written "strips" first began to appear in the *Voice* (he contributes them free), he has produced three best-selling books of strips averaging, I'd guess, about forty words to each page of drawings (*Sick, Sick, Sick; Passionella;* and *The Explainers*), a revue (also called *The Explainers*) in Chicago's Playwrights Theatre, and his first play, *Crawling Arnold,* a one-act satire which was performed last summer at Gian-Carlo Menotti's Festival of Two Worlds at Spoleto in Italy and which HORIZON herewith publishes for the first time. One of Feiffer's longer strips, "Munro," the story of a four-year-old who got drafted into the army, was made into an animated movie and won an Academy Award. Another collection of strips, *Boy, Girl. Boy, Girl,* will be published this fall.

Mr. Feiffer, now thirty-two, is reported to make an annual income "in six figures" (the kind of phrase he dislikes). He is a household word on college campuses, in London, and in Upper Bohemia generally. His work appears regularly in *Playboy,* a number of college dailies, the London *Observer,* the Paris edition of the New York *Herald Tribune,* and, through the Hall Syndicate, in newspapers of greatly differing political persuasions. His contract specifies that no one may fiddle with his wording; if a paper doesn't like what he says in a cartoon, it can skip it or substitute another, but the wording is inviolate.

Feiffer's strips are not comic strips in the usual sense; they are intended to wound rather than to amuse, though the blood they draw is in droplets. Feiffer is a compassionate satirist, and he uses his needle with a bedside manner ("I'm sorry, but this is going to hurt a little"), though he hopes to expose the basic ills of society and do what he can to cure them. He is at war with complacency, with the cliché mongers who provide society with meaningless slogans to live by, with the pomposity of officialdom, and with the carefully cultivated dullness of our carefully protected daily lives. But he wages his war by needling at the flanks.

In the segment of society to which Feiffer addresses his subtly wicked pen, the language of Freud is a sort of equivalent of the Victorian language of the flowers. Repressions, aggressions, guilts, Oedipal urges, and a profusion of other linguistic underbrush clutter the landscape in which his characters have their shadowed being. Feiffer's quarry is not those people who live on the hopeless fringes of life but those who live on the verge of attainable reality and who talk themselves out of ever coming to grips either with themselves or with their environment. They yearn, but they

TEXT CONTINUED ON PAGE 57

CRAWLING ARNOLD

A PLAY BY JULES FEIFFER

The scene is the expensively bedecked patio of the Enterprise home. BARRY *and* GRACE ENTERPRISE, *a vigorous, athletic couple in their seventies, enter with* MISS SYMPATHY, *a young and pretty social worker.* BARRY *and* GRACE *wear civil defense tin hats.* GRACE *wheels a baby carriage. All that is visible of the* BABY *is a small civil defense hat on its head.*

BARRY. Wait till you see the shelter! Spent over a year fixing it up! (*Offers* MISS SYMPATHY *a tin hat.* SHE *quietly demurs.*) You're making a mistake, Miss Sympathy. The drill will begin pretty soon.

GRACE. It's the only shelter in the country that has a television set and a whatayoucallthem dear?

BARRY. Sterco rig.

GRACE. Stereo rig. (SHE *begins to fuss with the* BABY, *making small gurgling noises at it.*)

MISS SYMPATHY. A television set? But what good would a—

BARRY. Yes—of course you understand it's not a real television set. It's the frame of one and then I have a 16 mm. movie projector and a library of films—Tim McCoy, Our Gang, Archduke Ferdinand's Assassination, Operation Abolition, Tony and Sally DeMarco doing the castle walk—a variety of fare. The idea, you understand, is that under enemy attack the family can survive down there for *weeks* while being able to simulate normal conditions of living. For example, I've had cards made up with the names of our favorite shows and at the time they would ordinarily go on we run a picture—a slide picture on the screen showing the *title* of the show—

GRACE. Lassie—Bachelor Father—Danny Thomas—

BARRY. And during the half hours those shows normally run we sit and reminisce about our favorite episodes. It's very important under crisis conditions to simulate normal conditions of living.

MISS SYMPATHY. You've *done* this?

BARRY. Tested it? Oh yes. Several times. Before Little Will was born Mrs. Enterprise and I—*and* Arnold used to spend many happy weeks—many happy weeks in our shelter.

GRACE. One gets to *know* Bachelor Father so much more deeply after one has talked about him in an air-raid shelter for two weeks.

BARRY. We have a library for ourselves down there, books and magazines. We have a library for Little Will—books for age groups from the threes up to the sixes. You understand, Miss Sympathy, *I* don't underestimate the persistence of the enemy. (HE *takes baby carriage from* GRACE *and begins to fuss with the* BABY, *making small gurgling noises.*)

GRACE (*proudly*). It's the only shelter in the country to be written up in *Good Housekeeping*.

MISS SYMPATHY. Little Will is how old?

GRACE (*proudly*). He'll be—

BARRY (*jealously*). He'll be two in September! (HE *buries his face in the blankets of the carriage, muffling the sound of his voice.*) Isn't this the biggest, baddest, toughest, little fellow who ever lived? I'll tell the world this is the biggest, baddest, toughest little fellow who ever lived!

MISS SYMPATHY (*peering into carriage*). My he's a *large* baby.

BARRY. Arnold was half his size at that age. Arnold couldn't crawl until he was almost *two*. Little Will's been crawling for four months now. *Four* months.

MISS SYMPATHY. And Arnold?

BARRY (*nervously*). Wasn't Millie supposed to bring us some drinks?

GRACE. Well, that's why we asked you to come, Miss Sympathy.

BARRY (*embarrassed*). Yes. Arnold is crawling again too. For four months.

GRACE (*sadly*). Regressed.

MISS SYMPATHY (*taking out pad and making notes*). That sometimes happens when the first child feels overcompetitive with the second child. *Sibling rivalry*.

GRACE. Crawl. As soon as he enters the house he falls on all fours and crawls, crawls, crawls. I say to him, "Arnold, you *know* you can walk beautifully. At business you walk beautifully—"

MISS SYMPATHY. At business?

BARRY (*embarrassed*). Arnold is thirty-five. (*Fusses with carriage.*)

MISS SYMPATHY (*making a long note*). *Advanced* sibling rivalry.

GRACE (*distressed*). That's what we wanted to talk to you about. I know there's nothing seriously wrong with Arnold. He's always been a good boy. Done everything we told him. Never talked back. Always well mannered. Never been a show-off.

MISS SYMPATHY (*taking notes*). He's never had any previous crawling history?

GRACE. I'm afraid he took the news of Little Will's birth rather hard. I imagine when one has been raised as an only child and has lived happily all one's years in one's parents' home, it's hard to welcome a little stranger.

BARRY. (*Buries his head in blankets, muffling his voice.*) Who's Daddy's brave big bandit of a man? Little Will's Daddy's brave big bandit of a man.

GRACE. Please, dear. Don't talk with your mouth full. (MILLIE, *the Negro maid, enters with three drinks on a platter. A coolness immediately settles in the room.* BARRY *and* GRACE *lapse into a sullen silence.*) (SHE *coldly receives her drink.*) Thank you, Millie. (BARRY *grumbles something under his breath as* HE *receives his.* MISS SYMPATHY *is obviously perturbed.*)

MISS SYMPATHY. (*Whispers to* MILLIE *as* SHE *is served her drink.*) I strongly sympathize with the aspirations of your people. (MILLIE *exits.*)

BARRY (*rocking carriage*). A nationwide alert! All the American people mobilized as one, sitting it out in shelters all over the country. That's what I'd like Little Will to grow up to see. I guess it's just an old man's dream.

GRACE. Here's Arnold! Please, Miss Sympathy, don't tell him you're here because we asked—

ARNOLD. (*Enters, crawling.* HE *is an attractive young man in his early thirties.* HE *wears a hat and a business suit and carries an attaché case.*) Father—Mother—(HE *notices* MISS SYMPATHY, *sizes her up for a long moment, then coolly turns to his mother.*) Company?

GRACE. Arnold, dear, this is Miss Sympathy. Miss Sympathy, this is our son, Arnold Enterprise.

MISS SYMPATHY. I'm pleased to meet you.

ARNOLD (*turning away*). That's O.K. (*to his mother*) Dinner ready?

BARRY. You're being damned rude, Arnold!

ARNOLD. I apologize. I have things on my mind. Are you having drinks?

GRACE. Oh, I'm sorry, dear. With you on the floor that way, I forget that you drink.

ARNOLD. Occasionally to excess. (*Crawls around.*) Did anyone see my coloring book?

GRACE. Millie! (ARNOLD *crawls around. There is an awkward pause.* MILLIE, *finally, enters with a drink.* MISS SYMPATHY *leans forward examining everyone's reaction.*)

ARNOLD (*accepting drink*). It's got an olive in it!

GRACE. Please, dear.

ARNOLD (*to* MILLIE). You know I drink Martinis with a lemon peel!

GRACE (*placating*). Millie—would you mind—(MILLIE *coolly takes back the glass and starts off.*)

MISS SYMPATHY. (*Whispers to* MILLIE *as she exits.*) I have great regard for the aspirations of your people!

GRACE (*to* ARNOLD). Did you have to—

ARNOLD (*to himself*). When I began drinking Martinis ten years ago, I ordered them with an olive. I didn't know any better, I guess. They always came back with a lemon peel. I hated the sight, aesthetically, of a lemon peel floating in my Martini. (*to* MISS SYMPATHY) There was something so garbagey about a lemon peel lying at the bottom of my Martini.

BARRY (*angry*). Arnold! I'm sorry, Miss Sympathy.

MISS SYMPATHY (*waving* BARRY *off*). No. No. I understand. (*to* ARNOLD) Please go on.

ARNOLD. (*Shrugs.*) There's nothing to go on. I got used to it. I got to like it. I got to *want* lemon peels in my Martinis. It still looked garbagey but I found that *exciting*! I've always been surrounded by lots of money, cut off from life. That lemon peel floating there in its oil slick that way was to me my only contact with The People. It reminded me of East River movies—the Dead End Kids. Remember the Dead End Kids?

MISS SYMPATHY. No, I'm afraid not—

ARNOLD (*suspiciously*). What do you *do*? (BARRY *and* GRACE *look distressed.* MISS SYMPATHY *warns them off with her eyes.*)

MISS SYMPATHY. I'm a social worker.

ARNOLD (*astonished*). And you don't remember the Dead End Kids?

MISS SYMPATHY. A psychiatric social worker.

ARNOLD. Oh, *you'd* remember Ingrid Bergman movies. Where's my coloring book, Mother?

GRACE. Where did you leave it yesterday, dear?

ARNOLD (*restlessly*). I've got to find my coloring book. I feel in the mood for coloring.

GRACE. I'll help you look, Arnold, if you'll just tell me where you think you left it. (ARNOLD, *perturbed, crawls around room looking for coloring book.* GRACE *follows him anxiously.* BARRY, *flushed with embarrassment, rocks the baby carriage almost violently.*)

BARRY. That's a good boy, Little Will, that's a nice, big, good boy, Little Will.

ARNOLD. I found it! (HE *crawls off in a corner with the coloring book.* GRACE *follows him. As* HE *begins coloring* SHE *looks over his shoulder.*)

BARRY (*miserably, to* MISS SYMPATHY). I've tried to know that boy.

MISS SYMPATHY. Communications between the generations is never easy, Mr. Enterprise.

BARRY. We wrote away to Dear Abby about him. She was snotty.

MISS SYMPATHY. I'm not sure you acted wisely. She's not licensed, you know.

BARRY. I tried in every way to get close to him like a father should.

MISS SYMPATHY. Perhaps if you had been a bit more patient—

BARRY. I've tried, believe me, I've tried. I introduced him

MISS SYMPATHY (*containing herself*). That's very good. (ARNOLD *shrugs*.) Do you mind if I crawl with you?

ARNOLD (*hotly*). Yes, I do!

MISS SYMPATHY. But *you* do it!

ARNOLD. I do it because I believe in it. You do it because you think you're being therapeutic. You're not. You're only being patronizing. I realize that in your field it's sometimes difficult to tell the difference.

MISS SYMPATHY (*with difficulty*). That's very good.

ARNOLD. If you really feel the urge to crawl with me—*really* feel it, I mean—then you'll be most welcome. Not any more welcome or unwelcome than you are now, by the way. I am by no means a missionary. Millie, for instance, is a missionary. She recently found an answer for herself and is appalled that the same answer hasn't occurred to everyone else. *She* has true missionary zeal. Like my father, she *knows*. You can't ever know in capital letters, K N O W, without also having to convert everyone else to your particular brand of knowledge in order to prove you're right.

MISS SYMPATHY. Basically all that you're saying is that everyone has his own point of view.

ARNOLD. If that's all I'm saying, it depresses me. Did you see my coloring book?

MISS SYMPATHY. When anyone says anything you don't like, you retreat into that coloring book.

ARNOLD. I admit it's rude. I shouldn't do it unless I have a coloring book for you, too. Do you wear glasses?

MISS SYMPATHY. Contact lenses.

ARNOLD. You'd be prettier with glasses. Or rather *I* think you'd be prettier with glasses. I like the way a girl looks with glasses. It makes her face look—less undressed. (*Waits for her to speak.* SHE *doesn't.* HE *picks up coloring book and begins to color furiously.*)

MISS SYMPATHY. You began to crawl at about what time?

ARNOLD (*distracted*). What? Oh (*absently*), when the baby began to crawl. "And a child shall lead them." (*Crawls a few steps.*) I'll tell you something that should interest you though—you being a psychiatric social worker—I had a recurring daydream—a fantasy—after Little Will's birth. It built slowly, but I embellished it day after day till it was a full-blown beautiful fantasy—the second full-blown fantasy I ever had.

MISS SYMPATHY. What was the first?

ARNOLD. The first? Oh, that was way before. When I was trying to lead a very active social life and I wanted to create an image of myself with girls—a lady's-man image. Funny, I haven't thought of this in a long time. (*He looks at her for encouragement.*) I had an idea—I used to have an idea about getting an answering service—starting up an answering service—I don't know why, but I find this a little embarrassing to discuss with you and it really isn't embarrassing at all. (*He waits for her to speak.* SHE *says nothing.*) Anyway it was a *special* kind of answering service where, no matter what time of night or day, the phone would be automatically answered by a lazy, sleepy, sexy feminine voice who'd sound like she was stretching every delicious part of her body and she'd say (*He yawns.*) "Who? Arnold? (*Yawns.*) Wait a minute, sugar, let me turn over and look. (*Yawns.*) No, he must

have gone out for bagels and coffee. Can I take a message?" I dreamt that dream with subtle variations for six months.

MISS SYMPATHY. And the other dream?

ARNOLD. In the beginning I thought it was obvious that the other dream—this second daydream I'm going to tell you about—rose out of resentment against the baby. Do you know how old my parents are?

MISS SYMPATHY. I hadn't thought of it. Middle fifties?

ARNOLD. They're both over seventy.

MISS SYMPATHY. And they had a *baby*?

ARNOLD. (*Shrugs, reaching for coloring book, changes his mind.*) My father doesn't look very much older than me does he?

MISS SYMPATHY (*evasive*). I don't know if I noticed.

ARNOLD. You're kind. But that's how it's been always. They're both alert, involved, aggressive people. So while I'm out trying, unsuccessfully, to make it with a girl and I come home, mixed up and angry and feeling like not much of anything, what are they waiting up proudly to tell me? *They're* having a baby. I'll try to say this in as uninvolved and unneurotic a way as I know how—it's hard to face a daily series of piddling, eroding defeats and, in addition, have the fact thrown in your face that your *father* at *age seventy* can *still* do better than you can. (*There is a long pause.* ARNOLD *fishes a ball out from under a chair and tosses it to* MISS SYMPATHY. SHE *one-hands it.*) You catch pretty good. (SHE *cocks her arm back.* ARNOLD *throws out one hand defensively.*) No, don't throw it. I'm not ready to compete yet.

MISS SYMPATHY. You were going to tell me about your dream.

ARNOLD. Well, at first I thought it was about the baby. I don't think so now, but it might be interesting to know what you think. The dream was about one of these baby kidnappings you read about every once in a while. (*A weak siren begins to wail erratically.*)

BARRY. (*Enters running, with baby carriage.*) That's it! The alert! Down to the shelter everyone!

GRACE. (*Enters with fire extinguisher and shopping bag.*) Oh, it's so exciting! It's so exciting! (BARRY *switches on a transistor radio.*)

RADIO VOICE. Stay tuned to this frequency. All other frequencies have left the air. This is Conelrad!

BARRY (*listening intently*). I met that fellow down at civil-defense headquarters once. You'd be surprised. He's just like you and me.

GRACE (*in a sudden, heated conversation with* ARNOLD). But you have to go down! You went down with us last year!

RADIO VOICE. It is the law that everyone on the street take shelter—

ARNOLD. We're *not* on the street. We're on the patio.

BARRY (*exasperated*). You think the Russians give a damn we're not on the street?

GRACE. It's the spirit of the law one should follow, dear.

BARRY. Arnold, I've had enough of this nonsense! Downstairs! That's a parental order!

ARNOLD (*hotly*). I colored the sky blue, didn't I? Why

don't *you* ever meet *me* halfway?

BARRY. (*Exits wheeling baby carriage.*) I can't do anything with him.

GRACE. We can't leave our oldest out on the patio!

BARRY. (*Re-enters with baby carriage.*) He's the one who's breaking the law. Let's go! (*Exits with carriage.*)

GRACE. You'd better follow me, Miss Sympathy. It's dark in the basement.

MISS SYMPATHY (*weakly, to* ARNOLD). It *is* the law.

ARNOLD. I told you I'm not asking for converts.

GRACE. For the last time, won't you come, Arnold? It's not going to be any fun without you. .

ARNOLD. I'm doing something *else,* Mother.

BARRY. (*Re-enters with baby carriage.*) The hell with him. The law doesn't mean a thing to *our* son. Come on! (*Exits with baby carriage.* GRACE *exits.*)

MISS SYMPATHY (*to* ARNOLD). I, as do you, question the sense of such a drill, but objecting to this law by defying it robs *all* laws of their meaning. Now I can see working for its reform while continuing to *obey* it, but to be both against it and defy it at the same time seems to me to weaken your position.

ARNOLD. They're all downstairs. You'd better go.

MISS SYMPATHY (*starting away*). You do understand?

ARNOLD (*dryly*). I think I hear planes. (SHE *exits running.*) (*sound of off-stage pounding*)

BARRY (*off stage*). Goddammit, Millie! What are you doing in there? Unlock the door! (*sound of pounding*)

GRACE (*off stage*). That's not nice, Millie! Let us in to our air-raid shelter! (*sound of pounding*)

BARRY (*off stage*). Millie! There is such a thing as the laws of trespass! You're in *my* shelter! (*Sound of pounding.* MISS SYMPATHY *enters.*)

ARNOLD (*grinning*). Millie locked herself in the shelter?

MISS SYMPATHY. She says "Let the white imperialists wipe each other out." (ARNOLD *laughs.*) I can appreciate her sensitivity and support her aspirations, but I reject the extremes to which she's gone. (*brightly*) But I do understand her motivations. (*sounds of pounding*)

BARRY (*off stage*). Millie, you're not playing fair!

ARNOLD. You really shouldn't be up here, you know.

MISS SYMPATHY. I thought we were having an all clear by default.

ARNOLD. I doubt it.

BARRY (*off stage*). All right, Millie. We'll stay down here anyway! We'll use the basement as our shelter! Down on your stomach, Grace. Where's Miss Sympathy? Miss Sympathy!

MISS SYMPATHY (*yelling*). Upstairs! I thought it was over!

BARRY (*off stage*). The law's the law, Miss Sympathy. We can't come up till we hear the all clear. Otherwise we'd be making Khrushchev happy!

ARNOLD. It *is* the law.

MISS SYMPATHY. What if I lay on my stomach up here? It's so dusty down there.

ARNOLD. I guess that would be *semi*-compliance.

MISS SYMPATHY. Does it seem within the spirit of the law to you?

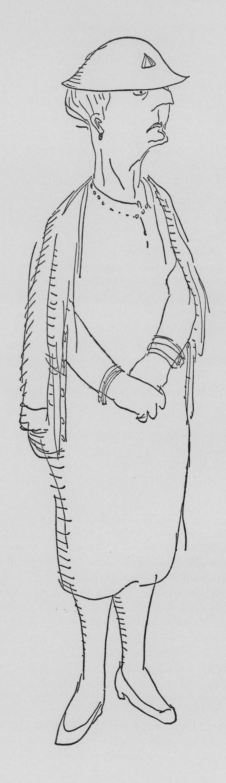

ARNOLD. Well, I know lying on your stomach *is* the accepted crisis position. I don't imagine you'd be penalized because of location. (SHE *lies on her stomach.* ARNOLD *views her with wry amusement.*) Don't you know how to stand?

MISS SYMPATHY (*dryly*). That's quite witty. You were telling me your dream.

ARNOLD. Yes, about the kidnapping. Well, you've read where there've been cases of kidnappings where the police suspected that the kidnapper was one of these lonely, child-hungry old women. Well, in this dream, *I'm* the baby. And I'm kidnapped. And it's a kindly, little old lady who kidnaps me. She makes all kinds of a fuss over me, but she seems rather helpless. She's had no experience with babies before, and she doesn't quite know what to do. Well, she turns on the radio, and what does she hear, this little old lady, but a recording of my mother, played every hour on the hour, informing the kidnapper that I'm a delicate child, given to head colds, and that there's a special formula she should make for me and there will be a moment's pause to give the kidnapper time to get a pencil and a sheet of paper. Well, the old lady conscientiously writes down the formula and feeds it to me steadily for two weeks until one day my mother comes back on the air and tells her, every hour on the hour, that it's time to be taken off my present formula and given a new formula. And for a couple of weeks the little old lady feeds me the new formula until she turns on the radio one day and my mother tells her I'm ready to start eating solids. And then she prescribes certain baby foods which the little old lady rushes out and buys.

Well, the weeks go by, and each week, every hour on the hour, there's some new recommendation from my mother, coupled with a plea that the old lady should give me everything I need but that she shouldn't spoil me.

By the time I'm five, my mother is on the air broadcasting, "Now is the time for Arnold to start to school. Be very careful in choosing a school." And based on my mother's instructions, I'm registered in school, I'm graduated, a career is chosen for me—and once a month, every hour on the hour, on comes my mother with advice about the clothes I should wear, how I shouldn't go out in the street too soon after a shower, how I shouldn't have to keep up with the other boys and stay out all night—every hour on the hour.

When I arrive at the age where I'm ready to think seriously of marriage, my mother interrupts all regular programming with a special recorded plea—"Don't let Arnold be in such a hurry. That girl isn't good enough for him." (HE *shrugs with finality.*)

MISS SYMPATHY. That's an epic dream.

ARNOLD. I like that you said that. I don't know what the dream is, but it gives it dignity to be described as epic. It seems a dream worthy of me now. While, for instance, if you had said, "God, that's a sick dream" (*shrugging*), it would have *seemed* like a sick dream.

MISS SYMPATHY. Will you tell me why you're crawling? (ARNOLD *crawls over to* MISS SYMPATHY.)

ARNOLD. I find that in crawling like a child I begin to act like a child again.

MISS SYMPATHY. Is that why you started?

ARNOLD. Possibly. I did a very childlike thing on the way home. I never would have thought of doing such a thing before I crawled. As an adult my values encompassed a rigid good, a rigid evil, and a mushy everything-in-between. As a child I've rediscovered one value I had completely forgotten existed.

MISS SYMPATHY. What's that?

ARNOLD. Being naughty.

MISS SYMPATHY. You did something naughty on the way home. Is that what you're telling me?

ARNOLD. I don't think I want to talk about it right now. I want to enjoy it by myself for a little while longer.

MISS SYMPATHY (*exasperated*). God, you're as hard to reach as a child! (*quickly*) I understand why of course.

ARNOLD. Why?

MISS SYMPATHY. First you tell me what you did today that was naughty.

ARNOLD. First you tell me why I'm as hard to reach as a child.

MISS SYMPATHY (*as if to a child*). First you tell me what you did that was naughty.

ARNOLD (*kidding*). You first.

MISS SYMPATHY (*as if to a child*). Oh no, you!

ARNOLD (*kidding*). I asked you first.

MISS SYMPATHY (*as if to a child*). Then will you tell me?

ARNOLD (*trying to withdraw*). Yes.

MISS SYMPATHY (*very arch*). Promise?

ARNOLD (*serious*). Yes.

MISS SYMPATHY (*very arch*). Cross your heart and hope to die?

ARNOLD. (*Stares at her, unbelieving.*) I can understand why you have trouble reaching children.

BARRY (*off stage*). Hey, up there—have you heard the all clear sound yet?

MISS SYMPATHY (*yelling*). No, it hasn't, Mr. Enterprise!

BARRY (*off stage*). Funny. It should have sounded by now.

GRACE (*off stage*). I'm getting a chill lying on my stomach this way.

BARRY (*off stage*). It's the proper position, Grace.

GRACE (*off stage*). Can't we go up soon, Barry?

BARRY (*off stage*). When the all clear sounds, we'll go up. That's the law. Is that Millie yelling something?

GRACE (*off stage*). Yell louder, Millie. We can't hear you. (*pause*) She wants to know if the all clear sounded yet.

BARRY (*off stage*). Tell her to go to hell.

ARNOLD (*after a long study of* MISS SYMPATHY). Do you really want me to get up?

MISS SYMPATHY. It's not what *I* want. It's what's best for yourself.

ARNOLD. You mean if I got up, I'd be doing it for myself?

MISS SYMPATHY. Not for me. Not for your mother. Not for your father. Strictly for yourself.

ARNOLD. That's too bad. I don't care much about getting up for myself. I would have liked to have done it for you though.

MISS SYMPATHY (*quickly*). I *would* be very pleased.

ARNOLD. If I got up right now?

MISS SYMPATHY. Yes.

ARNOLD. (*Begins to rise.*) O.K.

MISS SYMPATHY. NO!

ARNOLD (*on one knee*). But you said—

MISS SYMPATHY. Not *now*. *Later*! (*Whispers.*) It's against the law!

ARNOLD. (*Shrugs, returns to his crawling position.*) Did you see my coloring book?

MISS SYMPATHY. You're not being *honest*! You blame me for accepting the rules of society. Well, without those rules we'd have anarchy. Every mature person has to operate within the warp and woof of society. You want to operate outside that warp and woof, to return to a *child*'s world—to start all over again!

ARNOLD (*appreciatively*). Yeah! (*From his pocket* HE *plucks a lollipop.*)

MISS SYMPATHY. Well, you *can't* start all over again. It will all come out the *same* way!

ARNOLD (*sucking pop*). Then I'll start all over again again.

MISS SYMPATHY. But it will all come out the same way *again*!

ARNOLD. Then I'll start all over again again again. It's *my* game. (HE *takes a long loud suck on lollipop.*)

BARRY (*off stage*). Wasn't that the all clear?

MISS SYMPATHY. I'm afraid not, Mr. Enterprise.

GRACE (*off stage*). I'm catching cold.

BARRY (*off stage*). Let me put my jacket under you.

GRACE (*off stage*). I'm *tired* of this.

BARRY (*off stage*). But it's only a few minutes. We've spent over two weeks in our shelter.

GRACE (*off stage*). But we had television.

BARRY (*off stage*). The law is there for the citizens to obey. If *we* are irresponsible, how can we attack others for being irresponsible?

MISS SYMPATHY (*to* ARNOLD). You have a very irresponsible attitude.

ARNOLD. Naughty is the word I prefer.

MISS SYMPATHY. You were going to tell me something.

ARNOLD. I forgot.

MISS SYMPATHY. What you did on the way home from work—something naughty.

ARNOLD. Do you find me attractive, Miss Sympathy?

MISS SYMPATHY. Yes, I do.

ARNOLD (*surprised*). You can say it just like that?

MISS SYMPATHY. Because I do. I know I do. You're the kind of person I find attractive *always*. From previous examples I know you fall into my spectrum of attractiveness. (*a nervous pause*) Actually it's because I find you so attractive that I'm having trouble with you. If I didn't find you attractive, I could explain your problem without the slightest difficulty.

ARNOLD. Everything's so complicated.

MISS SYMPATHY. We live in a complex world.

ARNOLD. *Children* are complex. Adults are just complicated.

MISS SYMPATHY. Why did you ask if I found you attractive?

ARNOLD. Because we've been alone for a while and we'll be alone for a while longer. I thought it was the right thing to say.

MISS SYMPATHY. We have a time limit. The all clear will probably sound any minute.

ARNOLD. Four months ago you wouldn't have found me attractive.

MISS SYMPATHY. Why do you say that?

ARNOLD. Because four months ago I didn't crawl. Crawling has made me a more attractive person.

MISS SYMPATHY. It has? How?

ARNOLD. Well, for one thing, I'm conspicuous now. I never used to be. There's a certain magnetism conspicuous men have for women. (*more cautiously*) I *think* conspicuous men have for women.

MISS SYMPATHY. No, don't stop. In some ways you're right.

ARNOLD. I'm more assertive now. Everybody use to have *their* road. My mother, my father, my friends, Millie—with me the question was, Whose road would I take? Whose side was I on. Now I have *my* road, *my* side.

MISS SYMPATHY. You're terribly sweet. Do you mind if I crawl over to you?

ARNOLD. I'd like it. (SHE *does. For a while* THEY *stare wistfully at each other. Then* ARNOLD *drops to his stomach and kisses her.*) I'm on my stomach now.

MISS SYMPATHY. Yes.

ARNOLD. I'm not even crawling anymore. That's *real* regression.

MISS SYMPATHY. Yes. (HE *kisses her.*) Before we do anything I want to tell you—

ARNOLD. What?

MISS SYMPATHY. Before—when I was feeling sorry for you —I felt you'd rejoin society if you were only made to feel like a man.

ARNOLD. An expert analysis.

MISS SYMPATHY. I was going to offer to go to bed with you to make you feel like a man. I couldn't offer myself in that spirit now.

ARNOLD. I'm glad you told me. The social worker my folks had in last month went to bed with me because she wanted to make me feel like a man. I think she got more out of it than I did.

MISS SYMPATHY. How many have there been?

ARNOLD. One a month for four months. My parents keep bringing them around. They're very nervous about me.

MISS SYMPATHY (*doubtfully*). You're not just using me, Arnold—

ARNOLD. We're using each other, Miss Sympathy. That's what using's for. (HE *begins to unbutton the back of her blouse.*)

MISS SYMPATHY. The all clear—what if the all clear should sound?

ARNOLD. It won't. That's what I did that was naughty today.

MISS SYMPATHY (*sensuously, as* HE *begins to remove her blouse and the lights begin to dim*). What?

ARNOLD. I broke it. (HE *unzips her skirt. The sound of the zipper rings very loud.*)

BARRY (*off stage*). Was that the all clear?

(*Blackout*)

a "house for building" is what Walter Gropius called the new school he founded in Germany in 1919. But the Bauhaus was much more than its modest name implies: it was a force that changed the shape of the modern world. During the fourteen years of its existence, first in Weimar, above, then in Dessau, below, it created the patterns and set the standards of present-day industrial design; it helped to invent modern architecture; it altered the look of everything from the chair you are sitting in to the page you are reading now.

Picture credits:
Courtesy Herbert Bayer
Busch-Reisinger Museum, Cologne
Courtesy Walter Gropius

TEXT CONTINUED FROM PAGE 48

do not cope. They can always find an explanation, a way out, someone else to blame.

The most attentive audience for Feiffer's attacks is, by and large, composed of those whom he attacks most frequently. He is read by the pretentious and talented young, by the sociologically oriented and the psychically adjusted, and by advertising men who work in what they call (but nobody else does) the "creative" departments. The best clandestine audience for satire is not uncommonly the satirized.

Feiffer is a cartoonist by profession and a writer by temperament and talent. He has been compared to Goya and Hogarth, inaccurately; the comparison must have embarrassed him. His style, as he has said, owes something to William Steig and something to Robert Osborn, though it has become a personal shorthand and is of only minor visual interest. His drawings admirably serve his literary, sardonic, and humanitarian purposes, but he is not a man who, like Steig and Osborn, thinks first with his eyes. It would be inconceivable for him to say in a dozen drawings as much as a true visual satirist like Steinberg can say in a dozen lines. He is not, on the other hand, a gag cartoonist whose drawings are intended to explain a caption; his drawings work quietly with his captions, so unobtrusively, in most cases, that one is scarcely aware of them. They help to establish and maintain the mood he wants, and they make it possible for him to suggest place and time and character without having to define them further. It is said that he draws easily and writes painstakingly; in other words, he puts the effort where it is worth it.

The effect of Feiffer's strips, with their ten or a dozen drawings on a page or a single spread, is at its best that of the short story. He does not deal in anecdote, as so many cartoon strips do; he deals in vignettes or segments of life, suggesting with the economy of the short-story writer what has come before and must inevitably come after. Occasionally he uses an O. Henry sort of reverse twist with an elegance and precision that is shocking and epigrammatic. When he expands from a single strip to longer and more complicated series of drawings and captions, he leaves reality for fantasy; the satire tends to become watery and the comment sentimental. His talent, however, is not going to be contained by the fact that he has mastered a short form, as *Crawling Arnold* demonstrates. Any form, so long as it leaves room for his mordant needle, will serve him and, I suspect, will serve him better and better as he learns that the disciplines of elbowroom demand the same precision as writing in a strait jacket.

It seems unlikely that any young man of our day is to be so extensively explained as the author of *The Explainers,* a satire made up of cartoons which attack our contemporary necessity to justify ourselves. Feiffer, indeed, has already gone to a certain amount of trouble to explain himself to explainers and to interviewers. Like most good satirists—and he is a very good satirist indeed—Feiffer is sharpest when he is dealing with his own shortcomings. He has said that "the satirist is defeating himself when he reveals his true feelings," and by this he evidently means that the key in which he speaks must be lower than the key in which he feels. He has also said that he is "for hate, but against bitterness"; yet in reducing the key of his hate for publication, there often remains a taste of bitterness in his work. Perhaps aftertaste would be more accurate, for there is a "more-in-sorrow-than-in-anger" feel about most of Feiffer's comment. It has been said that Feiffer writes with his ear (he is an extraordinary parodist of conversation); it would be more accurate, I suspect, to say that he writes with his inner ear. He listens to his own heartbeat, his own voice, his own doubts, and often they are every man's.

Russell Lynes wrote about the work of Robert Osborn in Horizon *for September, 1960.*

the bauhaus

By WOLF VON ECKARDT

Sometime after their move to Dessau in 1925, the Bauhaus masters were photographed on the roof of their new building. From the left, they are: Josef Albers, painter, now visiting critic at the School of Fine Arts, Yale; Hinnerk Scheper, muralist, who died in 1957; Georg Muche, painter, now living in Württemberg; László Moholy-Nagy, painter-designer-photographer, who was director of the New Bauhaus in Chicago until his death in 1946; Herbert Bayer, painter-typographer-designer, now associated with the Container Corporation of America and also a practicing architect in Aspen, Colorado; Joost Schmidt, painter-sculptor, who died in 1948; Walter Gropius, founder and director of the Bauhaus, later chairman of the Department of Architecture at Harvard, and now, at 78, busier than ever as a practicing architect in Cambridge, Massachusetts; Marcel Breuer, architect and designer, now practicing internationally from New York; Wassily Kandinsky, painter, who died in 1944; Paul Klee, painter, who died in 1940; Lyonel Feininger, American-born painter, who died in 1956; Gunta Stölzl, weaver, who now has her own workshop in Zurich; and Oskar Schlemmer, painter, workshop teacher, stage designer, who died in 1943.

A typical Bauhaus workshop at Dessau

It was a motley crowd, unkempt and unruly, that flocked in the spring of 1919 to the picturesque mid-German town of Weimar—where, just then, the constitution was being written that gave the Weimar Republic its name.

They came from all over the country in those chaotic months after the German empire's downfall: boys in the blue shirts and leather shorts of the youth movement, girls from the art academies and craft workshops, and men pushing forty, still in the battered uniforms of the Kaiser's defeated army. All of them were poor; the hunger and the halfhearted revolution of Germany's last, bitter World War I winter still lingered on. And all of them were attracted by a ringing proclamation announcing a new school, a new training laboratory of art, architecture, and design, to be established at Weimar. It was to be called the Bauhaus, or House for Building.

The proclamation was a modest, four-page leaflet drawn up by the thirty-six-year-old Berlin architect Walter Gropius, who had achieved early fame as a revolutionary designer of industrial buildings before the war interrupted his work; and on its cover was an expressionist woodcut, done by the young artist Lyonel Feininger, American-born of German extraction, which showed a cathedral bathed in the rays of three stars. The stars were symbols of Gropius's announced threefold intention: to break down the "arrogant barrier between craftsman and artist," to achieve a new unity of art and technology, and to "conceive and create the new building of the future."

These were bold and sweeping words. Yet they came at a propitious time, when in Central Europe in particular most old values, tastes, and hierarchic pretensions were in disarray, and when a voice calling for a fresh marriage of art and daily life sounded like the voice of the prophet. And by the time the Nazis forced it to close fourteen years later, the Bauhaus had accomplished these imperious aims to an astonishing degree. Bringing together for the first time teachers and students in fields ranging from architecture, painting, and sculpture to furniture and industrial design, typography, stagecraft, photography, ceramics, and weaving, it exerted a profound influence on the shape of "everything from the coffee cup to city planning." From Finland to California and Japan, the pervasive impact of the Bauhaus can be seen to this day—not because of a "Bauhaus style," for there is really no such thing, but because the Bauhaus has so altered our concepts of the design of objects for everyday use. It *did* break down the division between artist and craftsman, and developed the new profession of industrial designer; it *did* achieve a synthesis of art and technology, and thus helped to create a new kind of everyday beauty; and in the functional steel-and-glass build-

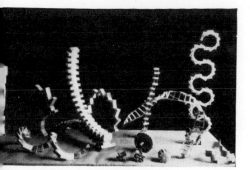

Construction of matchboxes

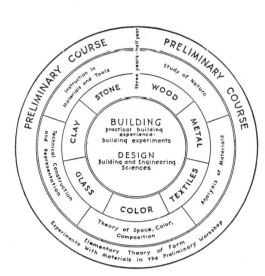

The Bauhaus curriculum

Cut from one piece of paper

ITS FRESH ATTACK

Before he could enter one of the Bauhaus workshops, a student was required to take its six-month preliminary course in basic design. Its purpose, said Gropius, was to "liberate the individual by breaking down conventional patterns of thought." Since the familiar ways of using materials were forbidden, a student was forced to strike out on his own. For example, paper had generally been used lying flat. And so, as Albers once explained, "we try paper standing upright, or even as a building material; we reinforce it by complicated folding; we use both sides; we emphasize the edge. . . . instead of pasting it, we try to tie it, to pin it, to sew it, to rivet it." Some examples of these experiments in the fresh use of materials are shown at right.

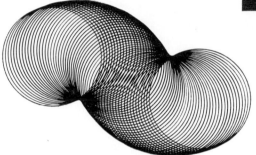

Study in optical illusion

ing of sometimes forbidding simplicity, which soon replaced Feininger's cathedral as the true symbol of the Bauhaus, it produced the dominant structure of our times.

That it achieved all this was due to the phenomenal array of rising talents it drew to itself, chiefly at Gropius's instigation. None were quite so well known as Gropius himself when they came; many were to be names of renown by the time they left. In architecture and furniture design, there were Marcel Breuer and Mies van der Rohe (the last director of the school before the Nazis closed it); in painting, Lyonel Feininger, Paul Klee, Wassily Kandinsky, and Josef Albers; in photography and other arts, László Moholy-Nagy; in the graphic arts, Herbert Bayer; and Anni Albers in textile weaving. Other artists less well-known in the United States, such as the painter and stage designer Oskar Schlemmer and the sculptor Gerhard Marcks, also passed some of their most creative years at the Bauhaus. And when the Nazis shut it down, many of these movers and shakers brought their talent and gospel to the United States: Gropius, to train a whole new generation of American architects, as Chairman of the Department of Architecture at Harvard; Breuer, to become another of America's leading designers; Mies, to head the architectural school at the Illinois Institute of Technology and also to become a major influence on American building as a whole; Moholy-Nagy, to found

the New Bauhaus at Chicago, which later was renamed the Chicago Institute of Design and which he headed until his death in 1946; Albers, to revolutionize art education at Black Mountain College in North Carolina and then to exert a powerful personal impact as Chairman of the Department of Design at Yale; Bayer, to set up new models of graphic design.

Six years after it was first established at Weimar, the Bauhaus moved to the provincial city of Dessau, with which it is particularly linked in memory. Yet wherever it was housed, it was never, as Mies has said, really "an institution with a clear program; it was an idea." And that idea began with Gropius.

Just a trifle bent now, in the latter half of his seventies, Gropius is still the "extraordinarily handsome German" that his first wife, Alma Mahler Werfel, describes in her memoirs. (The magnetic widow of the composer Gustav Mahler, she briefly drew the young architect into her turbulent life and soon left him to marry the writer Franz Werfel.) "[He] would have been well cast as Walther von Stolzing in *Die Meistersinger*," she wrote after her first encounter with Gropius.

That was in 1910. Gropius came from a family of moderately well-to-do Prussian state officials, artists, and architects with a strong liberal bent. He had started his career in the office of the architect Peter Behrens, where Mies and, for a short time, Le Corbusier also

61

Itten in Bauhaus uniform

Using the building itself as a stage

ITS LIVELY YOUNG MEN

From the outset there was a great deal of horseplay and improvised entertainment at the Bauhaus. Whether it was half-serious, like the bizarre uniform worn by Johannes Itten, or wholly frivolous, like the accordion-and-gunshot style of the Bauhaus band, it was all brilliantly inventive. Much of this energy was channeled into the stage workshop, where Oskar Schlemmer produced some startling mutations of conventional drama and ballet. He even toyed with the idea of a completely mechanized theater that could dispense with actors. But the Bauhaus theory that all the elements of a performance should be "merged into the higher life of the whole" is still as valid as ever.

Ballet on the beach, led by Xanti Schawinsky

were apprenticed. It was largely in Behrens's office that modern industrial architecture and design dropped the ornate twists of *art nouveau* and emerged in new, although still clumsily monumental, simplicity. And it was here that Gropius developed his strong interest in the German *Werkbund* (or "Crafts Association"), of which he soon became a prominent leader. This movement, founded in Munich in 1907, was striving to revive interest in fine workmanship—not in romantic protest against increasing machine production, like the earlier efforts of William Morris in England, but in an effort to reconcile art and industry.

After he had left Behrens and set up his own practice in Berlin, Gropius's first important commission in 1911 was to design a factory for the Fagus Works near Alfeld in north Germany. What he produced was the first major building in history to be completely sheathed in a smooth skin of glass. This was made possible by an interior steel framework which relieved the walls of the need to carry and support the structure, thus permitting them to be of hitherto unknown lightness and transparency. Later known as curtain walls, they served only to let in light and to keep out rain, cold, and noise. This innovation eventually led to the building of Lever House in New York (completed in 1952) and similar buildings of the so-called International Style. It launched both Gropius's reputation as an architect

and, in large measure, the twentieth-century architectural revolution.

Yet despite this immediate success, building alone did not satisfy him. He felt that the architect must lead his fellow artists in a collaborative effort to shape everything that goes into man-made physical environment. Thus, watching a funeral procession in Berlin before World War I, he was so offended by the sight of the ornate coffin that he immediately tracked down the undertaker and importuned him until he was commissioned to strip even this final shelter of the clutter of past ages. About the same time he also designed or experimented with a diesel locomotive, with sleeping-car and battleship interiors, an automobile, the industrial prefabrication of houses, and with new shapes and forms of furniture. "I made more money from the design of an iron stove than from all my architecture," he recalled of that period.

But Gropius soon realized that his vision could not be realized by one man alone. What was needed was a laboratory of design in which a new generation of artists could apply the discoveries of modern art to architecture and other needs of daily life. Such a new school would have to select talented young people, before they had surrendered to the conformity of the industrial community or had withdrawn into ivory towers, and train them to bridge the gap between the rigid thinking of the businessman and the imagination of

Dancers in Schlemmer's "Musical Clown," rehearsing on roof

Mask studies by Oskar Schlemmer

Scene from "The Circus," 1924

the creative artist. His first opportunity to realize this vision came unexpectedly in the second year of the war.

In 1915 Gropius was suddenly summoned from military service at the front to the court of Weimar, seat of a Thuringian petty principality that had prided itself on patronage of the arts ever since the time when its Grand Duke Karl August of Sachsen-Weimar-Eisenach in 1774 had invited the poet Goethe to his tiny capital and made him minister of state. Weimar had played host also to the poets Schiller, Herder, and Wieland, to Franz Liszt, to the first performances of many of Wagner's operas, and to Friedrich Nietzsche as well. It regarded itself, with considerable justification, as a center of German arts and liberalism. The reigning Grand Duke, whose establishment included a Grand Ducal School of Arts and Crafts founded thirteen years earlier by the Belgium architect-craftsman Henri van de Velde—one of the significant pioneers of modern applied art and architecture—wished to know whether Gropius would now take over its direction.

Gropius gave much thought to the offer, but it did not finally materialize until the war was over. When on April 1, 1919, the contract was at last drawn up by the office of the Court Chamberlain, it required and received the consent of the Provisional Socialist Government of the new Republic of Sachsen-Weimar-Eisenach.

The situation at the moment was parlous. While politicians at Weimar talked bravely of a new democratic beginning, homeless, disillusioned officers and noncoms of the defeated army were already talking revenge and sowing the seeds of reaction and counterrevolution. Yet there was a glow of high hope on the faces of the artists and intellectuals in the cafés and unheated studios of Berlin's Kurfürstendamm and Munich's Schwabing. Wedged between the Kaiser's fall and Hitler's rise was an extraordinary burst of German creativity—a time which produced great novels by Thomas Mann and Franz Werfel, paintings by Emil Nolde and Oskar Kokoschka, sculpture by Wilhelm Lehmbruck and Ernst Barlach, music by Arnold Schoenberg and Kurt Weill, drama productions by Max Reinhardt and Erwin Piscator, and enduring films by Ernst Lubitsch and Josef von Sternberg. "It was a period," Gropius reflected, "inspired by constructive ideas not yet subjected to the blight of frustration which overshadows the world today."

Gropius decided "to go whole hog," as he put it. He demanded that not only the Arts and Crafts School but also the Weimar Academy of Fine Arts across the street be put under his direction, and that these two state institutions be combined under the name "Staatliches Bauhaus Weimar." So great was the appeal that two out of every three of the first enthusiastic applicants had to be turned away.

Picture credits:
Courtesy "Magnum" Magazine
Courtesy Walter Gropius
Courtesy Herbert Bayer (2)
Museum of Modern Art, N. Y. (2)

63

Moholy-Nagy: "Construction A II," tempera, 1924

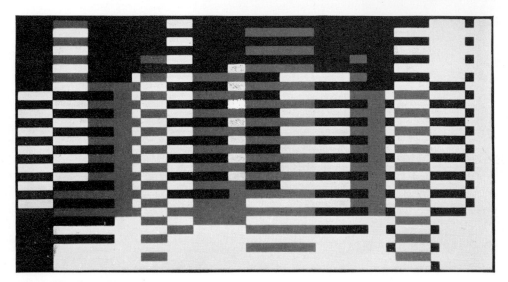

Albers: "City," sandblasted glass, c. 1928

ITS TEACHING PAINTERS

In painting, the Bauhaus is more celebrated for its faculty than for its students. No truly major painters emerged from the student body, even though among its teachers were such famous twentieth-century artists as Wassily Kandinsky, Paul Klee, Josef Albers, and Lyonel Feininger, as well as unclassifiable innovators like László Moholy-Nagy. The reason is: the Bauhaus was not an academy of painting or sculpture in the usual sense; its emphasis on the interrelation of all the arts tended to inhibit—as it was meant to—a student's developing along too specialized lines. But the teachers whose work is reproduced here had already arrived in mid-career; their course was set—they were painters. For them the Bauhaus was a place at which to develop along lines already chosen.

The Arts and Crafts building, designed by Van de Velde and located on the outskirts of the town, at first had room for only forty or fifty students. There was no tuition fee. Most of the students, like the faculty, lived in whatever quarters they could find in town. For those who could not afford the rent, Gropius got the authorities to provide a free dormitory. He also obtained some land on which the students raised produce for their inexpensive canteen, a vital necessity in those hungry days. Still, says Gropius, "I never knew how some of them made it."

Among the first art instructors whom he brought to Weimar were Gerhard Marcks, who took over the ceramics workshop; the strange, eccentric, and extremely gifted Swiss artist Johannes Itten, who developed the basic design course; and Lyonel Feininger, who taught only in the Bauhaus's early years but remained with it as resident artist until it closed. In 1921 Paul Klee joined the staff. Kandinsky arrived the following year.

The Bauhaus curriculum, at least during the Weimar period, was a rather haphazard affair, changing as new ideas turned up and special talents asserted themselves. But two central teaching concepts remained with the Bauhaus throughout: one was the six-month basic design course, which every student had to take before he could enter a workshop; the other was the adherence of the Bauhaus to the old crafts-guild training system. Each of its workshops had two instructors, a master craftsman and an artist, to train hand and eye simultaneously. Each workshop student had to sign a formal apprenticeship contract with the local trades council, an official body based on the guild idea.

The basic design course, although later refined by Moholy-Nagy and Josef Albers, was developed by the effervescent Itten, who liked to call it "the big house-cleaning of the mind," while his students often called it "purgatory." With tremendous verve Itten tried to make them forget all they had ever learned about art and helped them to discover their own spontaneous impulses and develop their sense of touch, color, and space. He would ask his students to draw abstract contrasts, such as thick and thin or big and small; he would teach them "the feel" of materials and texture by demanding meticulous drawings of wood grains and the like; or he would suddenly require the rapid assembly of collages made from odd objects.

Shivering in overcoats in winter, the Bauhaus students had to design everything they produced—whether in weaving, carpentry, metalwork, printing, ceramics, stained glass, or mural painting. Feininger taught in the printing shop, together with a crafts instructor. Kandinsky took over stained glass from Klee, who moved on to the weaving workshop and later switched to metalwork—where, as

Klee: "The Ambassador of Autumn," water color, 1922

one irreverent student put it, "he turned out spiritual samovars and intellectual door knobs."

Paul Klee was forty-one and well on his way to fame when he joined the Bauhaus faculty. "Klee still had a beard and wore clothes of unusual cut . . ." his friend and biographer Will Grohmann has written. "People with an eye for the unusual always stared at him. With his high forehead, dark brown eyes, hair combed forward like a Roman, and skin yellowish like an Arab's, Klee made a strange impression." The beard soon disappeared, though, and when Alfred H. Barr, Jr., of the New York Museum of Modern Art, met Klee in Dessau a few years later, he found this quiet and reserved man "the opposite of eccentric."

Kandinsky was somewhat taller and, with his rimless glasses, conventional attire, and slightly formal manner, looked more like the lawyer he once had been than an avant-garde artist. His first totally abstract painting, done in 1911, caused a sensation among the painters of Europe and was instrumental in changing the whole direction of twentieth-century art.

But even today, when artists like Klee or Kandinsky are far more widely accepted than they were then, it might seem to border on lunacy to hire them as government employees in a provincial town. "Nowhere else," writes the art historian Sigfried Giedion, "would

the director of a state organization have been permitted the freedom, given to Walter Gropius from the outset, to carry through such an uncompromising project and to call in the best talents from wherever they might be. On the other hand probably nowhere else would this have given rise to such violent opposition."

The opposition began as soon as the Bauhaus opened—abetted, no doubt, by the conservative academy professors whom Gropius replaced as soon as he could. There were posters and public demonstrations to "save our famous old art school" from these wild Bauhaus Bohemians and their capers. One day a bronze finger was cut off from the statue of Franz Liszt; another time a statue was painted green; yet even the policemen had to laugh when Gropius pointed out that an alleged molestation of a model in life class could only have been observed with a strong telescope from one vantage point —the house of an old spinster who lived cater-cornered from the studios.

Radically new ideas in art and art education, however, were no laughing matter for Germany's reactionaries. Gropius was continuously forced to defend his school against innuendoes of moral turpitude and political subversion. A charge involving his own morality persisted for years until he finally succeeded in taking it into a court of law, where he was promptly cleared. But how does one squelch

Text continued on page 68

65

Lyonel Feininger's early style had been brittle and congested, but at the Bauhaus it became spacious and romantic. This is his "Church of the Minorites, II," 1926.

Kandinsky's style took the opposite direction at the Bauhaus and became, while he was there, rather rigidly geometric. This is "Two Sides Red, No. 437," painted in 1928.

Moholy-Nagy: "Photogram," 1923

Poster for a Bauhaus exhibition, 1923

Text continued from page 65

the charge of "cultural bolshevism"? At an early date Gropius had strictly banned all political activity within his school; although here and there some student marched in a political parade, most of them held with Kandinsky who, much attacked in the right-wing press for compounding the offense of being Russian with the sin of painting abstractions, protested that he didn't even read newspapers. But a few Bauhaus people did wear a uniform at the time, a strange costume of their own design. This improvement over conventional men's-wear consisted of a kind of corduroy cossack blouse and funnel-shaped trousers, wide at the hips and tight at the ankles, and came in a wide assortment of colors. The rotund Itten and the tall painter Georg Muche, a combination reminiscent of Laurel and Hardy, once ventured to Berlin in this costume to call on a government agency. Itten was dressed all in purple like a higher cleric, while his friend was clad in silvery gray and resembled a giant carp. They never reached their destination: their appearance caused such a commotion on the streets of the capital that they were forced to take flight in a taxi.

Itten, it seems, was also responsible for introducing a bizarre gastro-religious cult called Mazdaznan. This sect can be traced back to one Mr. Hanish, a Californian of German extraction, who called himself H'a Nish, or something like that, and who grew a long black

beard, donned long white gowns, told his international following that he was a Persian prince, and preached his own version of the gospel of the good spirit Mazda of whom Zarathustra spake. His principal idea seems to have been that a pure mind will dwell only in a body kept clean by vegetarian food, including liberal amounts of garlic. The odor of this soon became so strong that people fainted of it at Bauhaus assemblies.

Gropius did not care much for this pseudo-Persian occultism but stayed above the battle. Itten eventually left to teach art in Zurich, Switzerland. The scent of Mazdaznan faded and for a brief period another "apostle of truth" took his place. This strange evangelist quoted Christ, Lao-tse, and Nietzsche interchangeably. Oskar Schlemmer, who introduced a lively dramatic and stage design workshop at the Bauhaus, described him in his diary for 1921 as a former champagne manufacturer who "now wanders from town to town, talking himself out of prisons and madhouses with great agility. I note this only because of his effect in Weimar: about twenty Bauhaus students declared 'Art is crap!', packed up and left southward without care or money." Later Schlemmer noted: "The Bauhaus is in a state of crisis. Another six students want to be off to Italy."

A state of crisis, however, was continuous at the volatile Bauhaus. Gropius usually calmed his critics by giving the students some special

68

abcdefghijklmnopqrſstuvwxyz

abcdefghijklmnopqrstuvwxyz

abcdefghijklmnopqrstuvwxyz

Top to bottom: German "Fraktur," classic roman, Bayer's "Universal" type

ITS GRAPHIC INVENTION

One of the first Bauhaus reforms was to clear the underbrush from the printed page. To that end its designers threw out all complicated type faces, useless ornaments, and—after 1925—even capital letters ("Why should we write and print with two alphabets?" asked Herbert Bayer). First to go was the archaic "Fraktur" type, a holdover from the Middle Ages still being used, up to that point, in virtually all German printing. In its own publications the Bauhaus switched to a form of roman and, ultimately, sans-serif type, like that in which this article is set. Layout was revolutionized, too, and all Bauhaus books, posters, and catalogues had a crisp, sparkling style that seems less dazzling today only because it has become so commonplace. Moholy-Nagy's experiments in photography resulted in "photograms," that is, exposures made on light-sensitive paper without a camera.

Bayer: Invitation to a Bauhaus costume party, 1928

task or responsibility, and when tension became too strong he would try to release it in some kind of entertainment. Even the completion of a particularly nice piece of work in one of the workshops would serve as an excuse for a party. In no time at all the students would rig up fantastic masks, costumes, and grotesque decorations. Dadaist posters would advertise these events, some of which grew out of the regular Saturday-night dances held in nearby country inns. Others, especially later in Dessau, grew into elaborate affairs in the best Mardi gras tradition, having themes such as "Slogan Festival" (with one girl appearing as "bare fact"). At the annual "Kite Festival" the sky over Weimar was filled with huge colorful birds, fishes, and strange abstractions. And on summer evenings the local burghers often watched a procession of paper lanterns in all shapes and colors winding its way through Goethe Park escorted by the dancing fireflies.

After Itten left, the Hungarian Moholy-Nagy took over the basic courses. A hectic, excitable man, he was as intensely intellectual as he was versatile, ambitious, and enthusiastic. There was little in the field of art and design with which he did not experiment, often with astonishing results. In Berlin he had pioneered in constructivism, a movement fostered by the Russian Kasimir Malevich which reduced painting to geometric symbols. At the Bauhaus and after, he turned

his boundless energy to experiments in type design and layout, photography, photograms (exposures on film without a camera), motion pictures, sculpture and product design in plastics and metals, exhibition techniques, and stage sets. He attempted everything, and often succeeded superbly.

At the Bauhaus, Moholy-Nagy was much criticized for his brash way of pushing himself into the foreground. Highly articulate and gifted with a journalistic flair, he became a sort of propagandist for the Bauhaus and edited most of its publications. Some derisively referred to him as "Gropius's drummer boy"; but in his writing, work, and teaching methods he probably contributed more than anyone else to the direction the Bauhaus was to take. His rejection of "soul-searching" and art "isms" helped pull the Bauhaus out of its early romanticism and save it from being just another art school.

Gropius tried not to interfere in what Schlemmer described as the "constant struggles, open or clandestine . . . [the] constant turmoil." He seldom asserted his authority; his tolerance bordered on deliberate permissiveness. "It was my approach to let it all grow," he recalls; "Foolish things would find their own end. I didn't want to risk squelching creative freedom." It was and is today the core of his philosophy not to impose his individual will on anything, but to give every new idea a chance and to strive for the synthesis of a

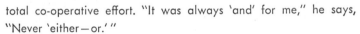

Poster for Werkbund exhibition, 1927

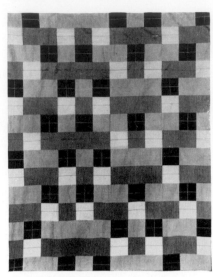

Anni Albers: Wall hanging, 1927

total co-operative effort. "It was always 'and' for me," he says, "Never 'either—or.'"

"Gropius's great gift is to let talented people rub their heads together until they emit creative sparks," one of his collaborators has said. "Then he keeps fanning these sparks until big ideas catch fire and something great gets done." Whatever general validity this personal method may have, Gropius has managed to make it work successfully for himself, both as an educator and as an architect. The highly personal idiosyncrasies of his peers, Frank Lloyd Wright and Le Corbusier, are totally absent from his buildings. He has done nearly all his architectural work—with some notable exceptions, such as the Bauhaus building in Dessau (see page 58)—in collaboration with others, among them Adolf Meyer, Maxwell Fry, and Marcel Breuer. And it is typical of him that his present firm in Cambridge, currently at work on a new university for Baghdad, should be named "The Architects' Collaborative."

At the Bauhaus, in the tolerant Gropius's words, it was Paul Klee who was "the final moral arbiter." And though his views differed from those of Gropius, Klee also sought to remain above the battle of personalities. Students sometimes referred to him as "the heavenly father," a nickname that reflected his aloofness from personal disputes and jealousies, indeed from all human foibles.

In contrast to Gropius's spacious vision of designing a better tomorrow, Klee turned to the microcosm of his tense inner world. "There is plenty of room left for exact research in art," he wrote, "but there is no substitute for intuition." As if to answer Gropius's thesis of orchestral collaboration and teamwork, Klee remarked: "Genius is genius, a state of grace with neither beginning nor end; it is generation itself."

Despite their differences the Bauhaus teachers got along well together and made it a point to introduce their many interesting visitors to each other. Among these were Stravinsky and Hindemith, with whom Klee established a close friendship. Yet in his prolific writings, except for his recently published posthumous diary, which ends in 1918 and in which he complains about some unsuccessful love affairs, Klee never refers to people at all, not even to his wife. Others unanimously report, however, that all who visited Klee's modest apartment, with its beautiful view over the park and its big grand piano, greatly enjoyed themselves. There he lived with his wife Lily, his son Felix, and an omnipresent cat. In conversation he would listen more than talk, and only once in a great while would he take his pipe from his mouth for a smile or a sage comment. Sometimes the Klees would play music for their guests; he was an accomplished violinist and Lily a pianist. Painting, he often said, was still

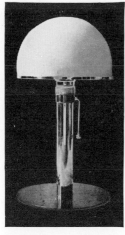

Wagenfeld: Lamp, 1924

Walter Gropius: Adler cabriolet, 1930

Josef Albers: Armchair, 1926

ITS DOMESTIC ARTS

The Bauhaus believed that it was "harder to design a first-rate chair than to paint a second-rate painting—and much more useful." By applying this principle as widely as possible, it gave a wholly new look to pottery, fabrics, silverware, lighting fixtures, furniture, wallpaper, even cars. Not all of these designs were first-rate, but the timeless elegance of the Albers chair at left is worth a great many second-rate paintings. The Bauhaus had declared war on nineteenth-century bric-a-brac; in a poster (opposite) designed for a 1927 exhibition it asked "Is this the way to live?" and gave its own answer by striking out the whole obsolete image.

M. Brandt: Teapot, 1924

far behind music in the arts; and it was his ambition to bring them a little closer. Klee's studio smelled strongly of a pleasant mixture of coffee, tobacco, glue, oil paint, expensive French varnishes and lacquers, and turpentine.

His Bauhaus lectures, only a fraction of which have been published, are phenomenal in their length and weight. One course alone —the "Secondary Aspects of the Circle"—runs to 426 pages. Yet the students enjoyed them. Klee would stand before the blackboard and, being completely ambidextrous, would explain complex matters while writing and drawing simultaneously with either hand, using chalks of different color. He never corrected a student's work but instead would sketch his suggestion for improvement on a small slate and quickly erase it again, leaving the student to work out the solution for himself.

"The object of the Bauhaus was not to propagate any 'style' system, dogma, formula, or vogue, but simply to exert a revitalizing influence on design," Gropius has stated. Nor did he wish the Bauhaus to have a "style" of its own. "That would have been a confession of failure and a return to that very stagnation and devitalizing inertia which I had called it into being to combat." The first Exhibition of the products of his scheme opened in the summer of 1923. At about that time Schlemmer received fifty million inflationary marks

as a birthday gift from his wife. He rushed out to buy a new shirt, which cost him twenty-four million. He took his change in five-thousand mark bills, a pile so high he could hardly carry it, but which he had no trouble spending within the hour—it bought him a book and a good meal. Meanwhile, the Bauhaus's Herbert Bayer was asked on a Thursday to design fresh paper money for the Treasury of Thuringia. As this money had to go to press on Friday, there was no time for any design except a typographic layout. When the new Bauhaus million-mark notes were distributed on Saturday, they were still wet with printer's ink and were sticking together. But inflation or not, the exhibition had to go on.

Fifteen thousand people, ushered by students in blue pants and white jackets, visited the show, which became famous in the annals of modern art in Germany. The week-long festival program included a performance of Schlemmer's "Triadic Ballet," an elaborate fusion of radically new stage and costume design and new concepts of dancing, which was to have considerable influence on the modern theater. On the musical program were works by Hindemith and Stravinsky. The Bauhaus band, a group of students who improvised Dadaistic rhythms on accordions accompanied by the pounding of chairs, smacking of tables, revolver shots, and other noises, played its peculiar brand of impromptu jazz for the dance. Herbert Bayer's

Picture credits:
Museum of Modern Art, N. Y. (2)
Courtesy Anni Albers
Courtesy Walter Gropius (3)

Gropius (and others of The Architects' Collaborative): American Embassy, Athens, 1961

exhibition posters were brilliant harbingers of some of the work this artist is now doing in the United States. The Bauhaus workshops displayed their first attempts to meet the challenge of the title Gropius gave the exhibition: "Art and Technics, a New Unity." And there was a building, too: a model house, known as "Am Horn," furnished down to the last salt-shaker with Bauhaus designs. Georg Muche, although a painter, had designed it, and Gropius assisted with the technical details. Many of the interior furnishings were designed and built by Marcel Breuer, then a Bauhaus journeyman.

But while supposedly culture-loving Weimar looked on, it was not pleased at what had grown in its midst. Gropius's difficulties mounted: rightists and Nazis gained increasing influence in the Thuringia legislature and cut Bauhaus funds by two-thirds, mostly on the grounds, it seems, that it had been launched under a socialist regime. To rescue it, a society known as "Friends of the Bauhaus" was formed over such a galaxy of names as Albert Einstein, Gerhart Hauptmann, Franz Werfel, Hans Poelzig, Marc Chagall, Oskar Kokoschka, Arnold Schoenberg, Adolf Busch, Edwin Fischer, and Peter Behrens. But in the last days of 1924 the frustrated Gropius announced to the Thuringian authorities his decision to close the school. The Bauhaus students decided unanimously to follow their teachers to whatever other place they might decide to take it.

Dessau, a small industrial city with some charming Gothic and Baroque architecture, bid successfully for it. Its far-sighted mayor, Dr. Fritz Hesse, provided funds so that the Bauhaus could have buildings of its own to house its studios and workshops, stage, lecture halls, students, and faculty. Gropius designed the new buildings. They turned out to be among the most remarkable and advanced of their time and embody what most people mean when they speak of "Bauhaus architecture."

The main complex resembles a somewhat stern but sparkling cubist painting. Still standing, in what is now the eastern German Democratic Republic, it is said to be in good repair and to have retained its original freshness. It consists of five boxes of different size, shape and material, which interpenetrate and because of their arrangement, seem to overlap. All seem to hover above the ground; one, an elongated horizontal cube in the center, is actually a bridge connecting the two main school buildings across a road. One of the buildings is entirely sheathed in glass—in the "curtain wall" manner Gropius initiated with his Fagus Works. Opposite is a building in sharp contrast: a solid mass on which the windows form bold, horizontal stripes. The wing to the rear which contains the student studio-quarters is gaily checkered with the shadows of strongly protruding balconies.

In its new buildings, the Bauhaus settled down to a brilliant burst

ITS MASTER BUILDERS

After their Bauhaus days, director Gropius and his successor, Mies van der Rohe, went on to become two of the most influential architects in the world. Both moved eventually to the United States, where their influence was exerted by teaching and example. Gropius became the head of the Department of Architecture at Harvard's Graduate School of Design, Mies the director of the school of architecture at the Illinois Institute of Technology. They made these into two of the nation's finest architectural training grounds. After retirement in 1952, Gropius returned to practice with The Architects' Collaborative. Mies, pursuing his theory that "less is more," has been designing structures of such spare but fadeproof elegance as the glassy Seagram Building in New York.

Mies van der Rohe

Walter Gropius

Mies, and Philip Johnson: Seagram Building, N. Y., 1958

of creative activity. Gropius thoroughly revised the educational program. The Weimar faculty, which had come along almost in a body, was supplemented by five former students: Herbert Bayer, Marcel Breuer, Hinnerk Scheper, Joost Schmidt, and Josef Albers, who now took over the workshops on their own. They had been trained, in Gropius's words, to be "creatively ambidextrous" and could replace the former double teaching by artist and craftsman. Leaving the Bohemian turmoil of Weimar behind them, students and faculty now lived closely but comfortably together. "There was a wonderful community spirit," the painter Xanti Schawinsky has recalled. "Gropius's architecture helped it along. All you had to do to call a friend was to step out on your balcony in the student wing and whistle." And Wassily Kandinsky wrote that he was so much happier than in Weimar that "even the movies don't attract us, and this is saying a great deal." For he admired Buster Keaton in particular.

Soon the Bauhaus received a considerable income from the sale of designs for industrial mass production. To develop them, students would work for short periods in factories to study production methods, manufacturing processes, and cost analysis. These studies, as well as a thorough understanding of the material used and the function of each object, preceded its design—in contrast to the work of many present-day American "stylists," who merely stuff their auto-

mobiles or other gadgets into beautifying shells in the hope of increasing their sales appeal. This is not to say that all Bauhaus designs are still valid. But they were thoughtful and mostly practical attempts to bring technical and functional requirements into harmony with aesthetics. Among them are ball-shaped lighting fixtures of the kind we still see in contemporary houses; glass-topped wood and metal desks which have largely inspired the currently popular Knoll and Herman Miller lines; chinaware and textiles as "smartly modern" as any advertised today; the tubular steel furniture which has at last mercifully gone out of fashion; chairs of which such latter-day designers as Charles Eames would even now be proud; and posters which would probably win a place in the next New York Art Directors' show.

With its name, the Bauhaus also brought along to Dessau its innate state of crisis. The town was doubtless more liberal than Weimar, but unconventional artists with unconventional ideas never lead a simple life. From the start, Schlemmer, who was given a chance to try some of his stage ideas on the local theater, complained that "even the ballet girls are afraid to be seen with us." Then Dessau's City Council, too, was changing its political complexion to the ugly brown of Hitler's storm-trooper shirts. The Bauhaus once more became a political football and its appropriations

Picture credits:
Megaloconomou Brothers
Charles Forberg
Morley Baer
© Ezra Stoller

73

American art and architecture would be a great deal poorer if Hitler had not forced the closing of the Bauhaus and driven to the United States the rich talents of Josef Albers, Marcel Breuer, and Herbert Bayer. As a furniture designer, Breuer created some of the indelible shapes of the twentieth century; today he is one of this country's leading architects, though his practice is world-wide. Bayer has had a major influence on the graphic arts in America, and has also produced some striking architecture in the Western landscape. Albers, first at Black Mountain College and then at Yale, has been one of the great art teachers of our time. Now semi-retired, he continues to paint those canvases which long ago became the ultimate refinement of geometric abstraction.

Breuer: Laaff house, Andover, Massachusetts, 1957

Bayer: Marble garden in Aspen, Colorado, 1957

Marcel Breuer

Herbert Bayer

were spitefully cut. And in a rare instance of mistaken judgment, Gropius appointed the Swiss architect Hannes Meyer to take over his architectural department. Meyer was a good designer, but also —as it turned out—an ambitious politician of left-wing persuasion. He attacked the fine arts in general and Paul Klee in particular and declared that the Bauhaus must serve the needs of the rising proletariat. Unwilling to cope with mounting intrigues and quarrels, Gropius resigned unwisely recommending Meyer as his successor. He was glad to return to private architectural practice. Herbert Bayer, Marcel Breuer, and Moholy-Nagy left with him.

Hannes Meyer's chaotic rule did not last long. In less than two years the city of Dessau asked Gropius to return to lead the Bauhaus. But he had learned to enjoy his independence and suggested young Mies van der Rohe instead. Mies quickly asserted his authority. The Bauhaus functioned well in the years 1930 to 1933 under his brisk direction. But the Nazi tide kept rising. Even before Hitler became Chancellor, Mies moved the Bauhaus to Berlin and turned it into a private school. This was of little avail. Nazi attacks on what they called this "hotbed of degenerate, cultural bolshevism" became only more ferocious. Finally Mies ventured into the lion's den and argued with Alfred Rosenberg, then Hitler's leading adviser on both cultural and racist matters. Although this top Nazi surprisingly promised to keep the Bauhaus open, Mies took the measure of his man and in a few hours closed it.

But the end could have been foreseen the evening Gropius resigned. At first the atmosphere was gloomy and the Bauhaus band refused to play. But Gropius insisted and a kind of slaphappiness took over. Suddenly the music stopped again. One of the students rose to make an impromptu speech: "You've made many mistakes, Gropius," he said, "but you can't leave us! We've gone hungry for this thing and we'll go hungry again. This is the end." Gropius replied in his precise, dignified way that, *in vino veritas* notwithstanding, the young man was in error; the idea would live on, regardless of people. At that point the students hoisted him onto their shoulders and there was such pandemonium that his further words were lost. He was probably trying to explain, as he did to me thirty years later, that the essence of this idea was to train architects and designers "who would bring beauty and unity into the chaos of our time." The idea has survived and flowered, though the chaos of the time remains.

Reared in Germany, and a student of the graphic arts and architecture here and abroad, Wolf Von Eckardt is with the American Institute of Architects in Washington. His article "The All But Lost Art of Handwriting" appeared in the September, 1959, issue of HORIZON.

Josef Albers

Albers: "Homage to the Square: Obvious," 1960

I Hear America Singing—Abroad

Numbers of our best young opera talents are starring in European houses. Yet they are denied a place at home

By WINTHROP SARGEANT

As nearly everybody who is interested in opera knows, American singers are invading the international operatic world in numbers that would have been considered fantastic before the Second World War. Statistics have been compiled showing that as many as three hundred and fifty young Americans are currently on the payrolls of opera houses in Germany, Austria, and Switzerland, where they are singing major roles and competing with enormous success against European artists, often amid some understandable grumbling on the part of European unions over the "Americanization" of European opera. It has been estimated that about 20 per cent of the singers now active in Central European opera houses are Americans, and though the percentage in Italy is somewhat smaller, it is still considerable. Moreover, these young American singers are frequently counted among the finest to be heard in Europe; the European public loves them, and they enjoy both the status of local celebrities and the modest but steady financial security that goes with the long seasons of work (often ten months a year) provided for opera singers in the big government-subsidized and well-attended opera houses of the continent.

For the moment, at least, they are in an artistic heaven, applauded, encouraged to do their utmost, and given what all artists really desire more than money: the opportunity to practice their art before a highly appreciative audience. Most of them look forward to returning to America to sing, and nobody knows how long the rather remarkable current hospitality toward American singers in Europe will last.

But the sad fact is that America, with its three or four fair-sized permanent opera companies (the Metropolitan, the Chicago and San Francisco operas, and the New York City Opera), is in no position to accommodate this new army of gifted Americans. These few companies, whose number is in striking contrast to the hundred-odd permanent opera houses to be found in Germany alone, have seasons that last (except in the Metropolitan's case) only a few weeks per year and do not offer anything in the way of permanent employment even to the few fortunate artists they hire. Thus, the American opera singer today is placed in a dilemma. He can make his way, with few exceptions, only in Europe. Americans are proud of his achievements, but not proud enough to provide him with a native forum for his talents—and, barring a complete revolution in our habits of operatic financing and production and an unprecedented efflorescence of public interest in opera, there does not seem to be much prospect of promoting this great reservoir of artistic talent on native soil. The American operatic audience has simply not kept pace with the American operatic artist, and a great cultural asset is in danger of being lost through public and official apathy.

Under the circumstances, one might ask how it comes about that Americans have taken to opera singing in such vast numbers when their native country offers them so few opportunities. A cynic might reply that Americans are more interested in singing opera than in listening to it, and it is true that, in general, we are a nation more addicted to ac-

The electrifying presence of James McCracken is caught in this photograph of him, as Otello, at Zurich's Stadttheater.

tion than to passive contemplation. But it is true also that America's operatic public is slowly expanding, that opera companies of a lesser sort are gradually taking root in smaller cities and in colleges, and that the future of opera in this country is not entirely bleak. The singers are ahead of the public mainly because they form part of the minority of Americans who take opera in deadly earnest. There has always been such a minority, and it is growing in numbers.

The history of the American singer presents an interesting record. There is nothing new about the existence of fine American operatic artists. We have had them for at least a hundred years, and the greatest of those in the past—Minnie Hauk, Lillian Nordica, Emma Eames, Louise Homer, Olive Fremstad, Geraldine Farrar, Rosa Ponselle, and Lawrence Tibbett, to name only a few of the most celebrated—have been international stars of the first magnitude. Up to the First World War most of them were women, and, being Americans, they were considered exceptional in a foreign-dominated and rather exotic environment. This environment, however, underwent a drastic change in 1935 when Edward Johnson, himself a great singer and a Canadian (which is pretty close to being an American), became general manager of the Metropolitan Opera.

Circumstances were peculiar during his administration. World War II raged during much of it, and foreign artists were not readily obtainable. Mr. Johnson, who had probably a more intimate knowledge of singing than any man who has held that post, searched the American scene for vocalists, and his remarkable acuteness as a talent scout enabled him to turn them up, without prejudice, in the most unlikely places. He did not have to depend on established reputations; he simply knew a singer when he heard one, and under his leadership the Metropolitan became, for fifteen years and for the first time in its history, a predominantly native institution. Some of the numerous Americans he hired were less impressive than others, but when Rudolf Bing succeeded Johnson in 1950, he inherited from him a very Americanized house and a group of fine American singers—among them Eleanor Steber, Nadine Connor, Dorothy Kirsten, Helen Traubel, Patrice Munsel, Regina Resnik, Astrid Varnay, Blanche Thebom, Risë Stevens, Martha Lipton, Margaret Harshaw, Richard Tucker, Jan Peerce, Charles Kullman, Eugene Conley, Barry Sullivan, Leonard Warren, Robert Merrill, Hugh Thompson, Mack Harrell, Osie Hawkins, Frank Guarrera, and Jerome Hines. Several of these singers developed into artists of unique stature and have remained among the outstanding figures of Bing's era.

It is difficult to overestimate the importance to America of the revolution Mr. Johnson brought about. He promoted the American singer to a position no longer exceptional but basic to the company's structure. He encouraged countless Americans to take up opera singing as a career, by opening the gates of the Metropolitan to the most successful of them. The singers I have mentioned, along with a large number of

Baritone Heinz Blankenburg (above, rehearsing Figaro) resides in Hamburg but remarks, "If the Met asked me to give it up, I could leave in a couple of days." Soprano Sylvia Stahlman (below, in her apartment with her mother) is a leading singer at Frankfurt's Grosses Haus.

American operatic talent in Europe is concentrated at Zurich. On stage at its Stadttheater, assembled clockwise around director Herbert Graf (with score): soprano Jean Cook, baritone Robert Kerns, tenor Glade Peterson, soprano Virginia Gordoni, mezzo Sandra Warfield, conductor Samuel Krachmalnick, coloratura Reri Grist, contralto Mary Davenport, tenor Robert Thomas, stage director Lofti Mansouri, tenor James McCracken. Each singer is costumed for a favorite role.

Page Swift (above, visiting Munich's new opera house) went to Europe as a Fulbright scholar and has become a leading soprano at Oberhausen. Regina Resnik and Phyllis Curtin (right, at the Café Sacher near Vienna's Staatsoper, where each has starred) are two American sopranos with important reputations at home who have won even more acclaim in Europe.

others who did not remain in the company as long, formed the advance guard of the present generation. The bars against all but the most spectacular American singers, which had existed in the days of Giulio Gatti-Casazza (general manager of the Metropolitan from 1908 to 1935), were down. Americans for the first time found in opera a normal, professional career, open not only to the few with extraordinary voices but also to those who, less magnificently endowed, had gifts that were valuable in the lesser roles which theretofore had been sung almost exclusively by Europeans.

The present phenomenon is to a great extent the result of Johnson's policy. Young Americans ceased to regard operatic success as a rare and freakish adventure into alien territory. They lost their feeling of inferiority. They discovered that they had gifts which made them equal, and sometimes superior, to Europeans. They were, in general, more resourceful and versatile, and sometimes more intelligent. They mastered not one but several languages and often sang equally well in Italian, French, and German. As a rule, they sang Italian opera better than most Germans did and German opera better than practically any Italians. They were conscientious workers and well-trained musicians, and their lack of respect for the sanctified and sometimes rather stuffy traditions of the European operatic ranks made them willing and eager to tackle almost any task, performing it with a degree of readiness and efficiency that surprised many Europeans.

It is no wonder that they took Europe by storm. They invaded a continent culturally disturbed and wearied by war, a continent that had lost a great many potential artists in battle. They were not always equal to the greatest European artists, but they helped fill a void, and thanks to the hospitality shown Americans in postwar Europe and to the fervent love of opera there, they found a place to work and shine. Today in Central Europe the words "American opera singer" carry something of the glamour and arouse something of the expectancy that the words "Italian opera singer" did in America a generation ago, and this, considering that opera is still a somewhat exotic and largely imported art in their home country, is a remarkable thing.

Where all this will end is anybody's guess. The Metropolitan, though it continues to hire Americans, is, under Rudolf Bing's administration, no longer quite the national institution it became under Mr. Johnson. Whatever Mr. Bing's virtues in other respects—and they are unquestionably considerable—he is more cautious and less oriented to this side of the ocean than his predecessor; and he has often been guilty of hiring mediocre Europeans with reputations, while slighting much abler though perhaps less celebrated Americans. Frequently an American singer—James Mc-Cracken is a good example—has been limited to minor roles at the Metropolitan and has subsequently left for Europe to become a top-ranking singer there. In other cases—Phyllis Curtin may serve as an example here—a singer who has been denied entrance to the Metropolitan on the basis her artistry deserves has gone off to Europe to achieve triumphs in Vienna and elsewhere. The casting policies of the Metropolitan in this respect have been questioned by many and undoubtedly ought to be thoroughly aired. But whatever the Metropolitan's oversights and errors may be, the fact remains that it is in no position to take over the bulk of the American talent that is currently flourishing in Europe. It is, after all, only one opera house, with a roster of some ninety principal singers, and its season, though long by American standards, is short compared with the seasons of the opera houses of Europe. The only solution would seem to be: more American opera houses.

Many people are worrying about this problem. One of the most conscientious thinkers about it is Herbert Graf, an Austrian long active as stage director of the Metropolitan under both Johnson and Bing and now impresario of Zurich's Stadttheater, which he has turned into pretty much of an American opera house (see top of page 79). Graf is a great enthusiast about American singers and delights in discovering and training them. A short time ago, with the help of the Rockefeller Foundation, he published a lengthy diagnosis of the plight of opera in America. One of his valuable recommendations was that short opera seasons be grafted onto the annual activities of our hundreds of symphony orchestras. The idea is a remarkably practical one, since we are as rich in orchestras as we are poor in opera companies; and it is not at all inconceivable that the average auditor, tired of endless repetitions of Beethoven's Fifth Symphony, might find himself intrigued by an occasional performance of *Carmen* or *Così Fan Tutte* for a change.

This idea seems to offer a fairly promising way out of our young singers' difficulties, as well as a possible arena for the increasing number of American opera composers, who are perhaps the most vital group now engaged in the creation of American music of any sort. In the end everything, of course, depends on public support. The American musical audience is primarily an audience of symphony concertgoers and has not as yet realized the enormous pleasure and satisfaction that is to be had from opera, which is, of course, by no means the lesser of the two arts. All that it needs is a bit of indoctrination. Give the average sensitive music lover a taste of opera; let him come to appreciate its magnificent music and its drama, lofty or trivial; introduce him to the peculiar excitement that comes from the sporting connoisseurship of singers—from comparing their abilities as one would compare great baseball pitchers—and you will have hooked him for life as an opera fan. Most people who profess to dislike opera are simply not very well acquainted with it.

Winthrop Sargeant, who contributed "New Life in the Old Opera House" to Horizon *for January, 1960, is music critic of* The New Yorker. *Among his books is* Listening to Music.

PHOTOGRAPHED FOR HORIZON BY EUGENE COOK

American singers have a flair for acting: Zurich has witnessed a moving Traviata *with Virginia Gordoni and Glade Peterson (above), and a glittering* Midsummer Night's Dream *with the stylish byplay of baritone James Pease and soprano Gloria Davy.*

A newcomer to Europe, Reri Grist had gained prominence in America before joining Graf's company in 1960. Above, she studies for her role as Despina in the Zurich production of Mozart's Così Fan Tutte. *Below, in a studio at the Stadttheater, James McCracken and his wife, Sandra Warfield, rehearse* Samson and Delilah *under the ebullient direction of conductor Samuel Krachmalnick and the startled gaze of a passer-by.*

CARDINAL MAZARIN'S FAREWELL TO HIS PAINTINGS

This year is the three hundredth anniversary of the death of Cardinal Mazarin, the real ruler of France during the boyhood of Louis XIV and one of the greatest collectors in the history of art. To mark the occasion the French government has reassembled many of his treasures in a sumptuous exhibition at the Bibliothèque Nationale, which was once the Cardinal's private palace. It was here, a few days before Mazarin's death, that the Duc de Brienne witnessed a scene to touch the heart of any collector. This is his account:

"I was strolling through the new apartments of the palace. I stopped in the small gallery where one sees the woolen tapestry representing Scipio executed from the cartoons of Giulio Romano; it had belonged to the Maréchal de Saint André. The Cardinal did not possess a finer one. . . . I heard him coming from the shuffling of his slippers which he dragged along the floor like a man who is very weak. I hid behind the tapestry and I heard him saying, 'I must leave all that.' He stopped and paused at every step because he was very feeble, turning first to one side and then to the other and casting his eyes upon the objects which appeared before him. He said from the depths of his heart, 'I must leave all that,' and turning around he added, 'And also that. What terrible efforts it has cost me to acquire those things. Can I leave them? Can I abandon them without regret? . . . I shan't see them any more where I am going.' I heard his words very distinctly, they touched me, possibly more than they might have touched the Cardinal himself. . . . I gave a deep sigh and he heard me. 'Who is that?' 'It is I, Mon Seigneur, who am awaiting Your Eminence with a letter of great importance which I have just received.' 'Come closer, come closer,' he said in a sad voice. He was undressed, wearing a wrapper of camel's hair trimmed with fur and his nightcap. He said, 'Give me your arm, I am feeble. I can no longer do anything.' 'Your Eminence would do well to sit down,' I said and was about to take him a chair. 'No,' he said, 'I am better off walking. I have things to do in my library.' I gave him my arm and he leaned against me. He did not want me to speak to him of business. 'I am no longer,' he said, 'in a condition to listen to those things. Talk to the King and do whatever he tells you. I have many other things in my head at the present time.' And coming back to his original thought, 'Look, my friend,' he said, 'at that beautiful picture by Correggio and again at that *Venus* of Titian's and at Carracci's incomparable *Deluge* for I know that you like pictures and that you understand them well. Good bye, dear pictures that I have loved so well and which have cost me so very much.' "

In this contemporary engraving Mazarin is seen sitting outside the top gallery of his palace. Part of his collection is visible in the background. Other objects from the collection are, below left to right: the tapestry behind which the Duke hid; Titian's Venus; *a Correggio,* The Mystic Marriage of Saint Catherine; *Gentileschi's* Holy Family; *Raphael's* Baldassare Castiglione; *Carracci's* Deluge.

NEW TREASURES
FROM SUMER'S HOLY CITY

At Nippur, religious center of the

world's oldest civilization, American

archaeologists have unearthed a trove

of sculpture dating from 2700 B.C.

At Nippur, the holy city of ancient Sumer, an
American archaeological expedition recently
unearthed one of the richest and most important Mesopotamian finds in a quarter century
—more than fifty pieces of Sumerian sculpture
dating from about 2700 B.C., in the Early Dy-
nastic period of the oldest civilization known
to man. Some of the finest examples are reproduced on these pages by courtesy of the
joint sponsors of the dig, the Oriental Institute of the University of Chicago and the
American Schools of Oriental Research.

The Sumerians were perhaps the earliest of
the peoples of Mesopotamia, the "cradle of
civilization" between the Tigris and Euphrates
rivers in what is today Iraq. They settled in
the marshlands near the Persian Gulf at least
six thousand years ago, developed a flourishing agricultural civilization based on an elaborate network of irrigation canals, invented
a system of cuneiform writing, and by the
third millennium B.C. produced such city-
states as Ur, Eridu, Lagash, and their religious center, Nippur.

Situated on a branch of the Euphrates some
one hundred miles southeast of present-day
Baghdad, Nippur was regarded as the abode
of Enlil, god of the elements and highest deity
in the Sumerian pantheon. In its extensive
temple area, containing the shrines of various
gods, the recent trove of sculpture was discovered. It lay beneath the mud-plaster floor of
a temple dedicated to Inanna, goddess of love
and war. On higher and lower levels of this
site are traces of similar structures, indicating
that the temple of Inanna was repaired and
rebuilt time and again, each new sanctuary
atop the ruins of its predecessor, over nearly
three thousand years—or longer than the entire span of Western history since Homer.

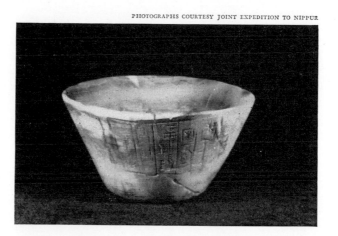

The Sumerians are credited with inventing the art of
writing, and this alabaster bowl contains one of their
early inscriptions—a dedication to the goddess Inanna
written in pre-cuneiform pictographs. The tiny stone
head below, here represented nearly twice its actual
size, has the geometrical roundness and prominent
eyes that characterize the earliest Sumerian sculpture.
The inlaid shell-and-lapis-lazuli eyes suggest that
the Sumerians darkened their own eyes with kohl.

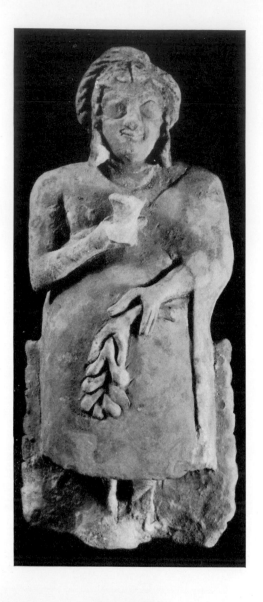

Most spectacular of the recent finds at Nippur is the five-inch statuette opposite, made of translucent gypsum. Its expressive gold mask, with the Mona Lisa smile that appears on much Sumerian sculpture, was originally attached to a wooden head, long since disintegrated; its finely carved body, poised in an attitude of suppliance, shows the bare-shoulder garment worn by Sumerian women. Some fifty centuries ago the statuette was placed at the temple altar by a woman—presumably a wealthy one—to represent herself permanently before Inanna. The stone figurines to the left served the same purpose: at bottom left is a rare double statuette of a husband and wife; at top left, a woman holding a cup and palm branch. Simpler stone figures (the head on page 85 may have belonged to one) were produced in quantity by Nippur's craftsmen. The steatite vase below, decorated with an intertwined leopard and snake with mother-of-pearl spots, was also an offering to Inanna.

These ancient works of sculpture express the guiding principle of Sumerian life—reverence for the gods. The temple was the center, often literally the geographic center, of all activity in the city-state, and man's every effort was a form of service to the gods. They, for their part—manifesting themselves mainly in the elements, which in Sumer are almost intolerably severe—were felt to be indifferent to the fate of mortals. Man could only hope to live in harmony with their incomprehensible decrees. His attitude, historians speculate, must have been one of grateful submissiveness —and may be reflected in the enigmatic smiles of these worshipers before Inanna. Their mystery and beauty are as old as civilization itself.

He can be seen both as a climactic figure of the Middle Ages and as a herald of the Renaissance. The first great realist in French art, he painted with magical perfection in a time of change and disarray

THE
ILLUMINATION
OF
JEAN FOUQUET

By MARSHALL B. DAVIDSON

In his lifetime Jean Fouquet of Tours was widely recognized as the foremost French painter of his day. If, as the records indicate, he was the bastard child of a priest and an unmarried woman, neither his reputation nor his career suffered on that count. His obvious talent won him the patronage of two successive kings of France, Charles VII and Louis XI, and he enjoyed favor in court circles as a matter of course.

It might have been a royal commission that took him to Rome as a young master in the mid-1440's to paint a portrait of Pope Eugenius IV. At the time, in any event, Charles VII was doing his best to heal the "pestilential and horrible" schism that for some years had left the Western Church with two popes who, "each with a doubtful title, made all Europe ring with their mutual invectives and anathemas." By supporting the Roman claimant as the true shepherd, Charles helped to mend the rift and, at a critical point in the affairs of his kingdom, added to his own luster as the "Very Christian King of France."

Some years later the Florentine architect and sculptor Antonio Filarete, recalling the almost magically lifelike realism of Fouquet's papal portrait (*che veramente parevano vivi proprio*), recommended him to Duke Francesco Sforza as one of the most advanced talents of the time. Fifteen years still later another cultivated Florentine who paid an extensive visit to Tours, and presumably knew Fouquet's more mature work, reported back to Italy with almost fanatical admiration that this remarkable Frenchman excelled all masters, past or present— that he could even rival Prometheus in creating the semblance of human life out of inert materials.

Contemporary judgments of this kind, even from the most respectable sources, are not always dependable. The history of art is littered with the frayed remnants of reputations that once seemed proof against the wear and tear of time. Fouquet's name was fondly remembered for some years after his death. Then for three centuries it was virtually forgotten, his work lost in anonymity. During the past hundred years

or so, however, what remained of his paintings and drawings has gradually been brought back to light, and the long fade-out seems to have done small damage to his fame. Lamentably little of his total output has been rediscovered, but half a millennium after he laid down his brushes, there seems ample reason to remember Fouquet with something close to the high regard he enjoyed while he was still living. Fortunately, forty superb fragments of what must have been his major work, the exquisite Book of Hours he illuminated for the royal treasurer, Etienne Chevalier, reappeared on the Swiss market in 1805 and were bought on the spot by Georges Brentano for 5,000 francs. Eighty-six years later these were resold to the Duc d'Aumale for 250,000 francs and deposited in the Musée Condé at Chantilly. The reproductions on the following pages (very slightly larger than actual size) are a selection from these precious remnants.

Fouquet *was* a Promethean figure. From our point in time we recognize him as the first great realist of French art, the founder of an enduring tradition, a painter whose name may be mentioned in the same breath with the great early Netherlandish masters, the brothers Van Eyck and Rogier van der Weyden. Whether that makes him a climactic figure of the Middle Ages or a herald of the approaching Renaissance presents a sharp question we need not settle here. Both those terms are inventions of a later day, contrived to facilitate our study of the past; neither would have meant anything to Fouquet. Men have always lived in "modern" times (although none have ever been so acutely self-conscious about this as we are today), and Fouquet was in every sense a man of his times.

It was a period that in retrospect seems to have offered little enough encouragement to the arts. Like his contemporary François Villon, the first great lyrical writer of France, Fouquet grew to maturity during the last miserable decades of the Hundred Years War, while France suffered a murderous cycle of strife and brigandage, pestilence and

TEXT CONTINUED ON PAGE 97

On the following pages: a portfolio in gravure from Fouquet's Book of Hours

ꟲV NATVS ÉET IHꟲ IBETHLEEM IVꟲE TOIEBVS ꟴERODIS RE

MAISTRE · ESTI · ENNE · CHEVALIER

TEMD · ILVM · BLON AC...

EV LAOIVTORIV MEV ſENOE ONE AO AOIWANOV

DEVS INADIVTORIV MEVM TENOE ONE HO AOIV

THE FUNERAL OF ETIENNE CHEVALIER

JOB AND HIS COMFORTERS

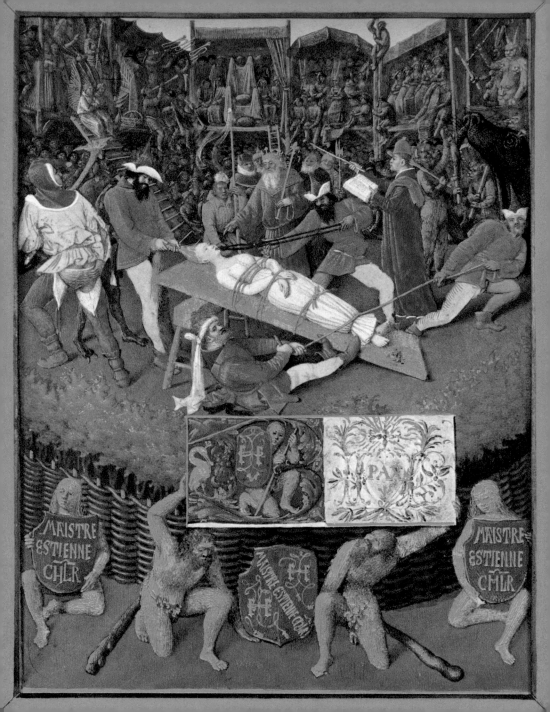

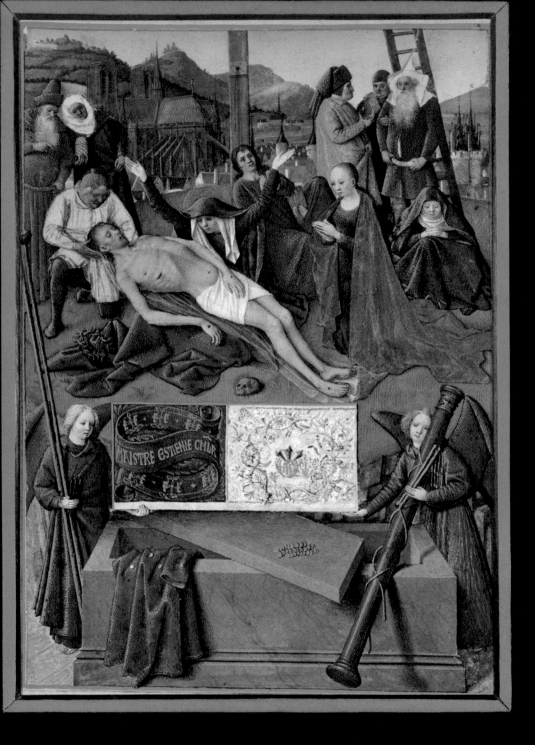

PIETA

famine. Trade and commerce had come to a standstill. Merchants took to the road only if they were armed to the teeth. In one grim year, at least, about the time of Fouquet's birth, no harvest reached Paris from the surrounding countryside. Instead, by day and by night, wolves drifted into the city precincts to scratch for freshly buried cadavers. Divided within itself, harassed by English invaders, and beset by unpaid roving mercenaries from both camps, France was for a while as close to complete ruin and anarchy as it was ever to be.

Yet even during those ghastly decades the sun still shone in France and the human spirit did not wither. At the court of the independent dukes of Burgundy; in the lands of Philip the Bold; in and about the little city of Bourges, where early in the fifteenth century the Duc de Berry commissioned and bought exquisite masterpieces and where Charles VII found haven from the divisive and oppressive forces that threatened his rump of a kingdom—in those and other scattered centers the arts had not been neglected. Even in Paris, with its English garrison, new, flamboyant structures were built; and here, in the atelier of some unidentified master was fashioned for the English regent, the Duke of Bedford, his magnificent illuminated Breviary.

It may have been in such a workshop that Fouquet learned his art. No one knows. Perhaps because of his illegitimacy the story of his earlier years remains obscure. By the time he returned from his several years in Italy, well-known and in full command of his genius, France had all but recovered from its long ignominy. At the battle of Formigny in 1450, two years after the schism within the Church had been settled, the English were in effect kicked out of France, to rudely paraphrase Joan of Arc's prayer. The defeat, *"moulte grande et moulte horrible,"* at Crécy almost a century before, the bitterness of Agincourt in 1415, could be forgotten, and from the decay of the past came new life.

Charles VII was aptly called "the well-served." As one historian wrote, he borrowed the sword of Joan of Arc and the money of the wealthy financier Jacques Coeur to deliver his kingdom from the English. He drew on both the material resources and the brains of the rising bourgeoisie to invigorate and reorganize his state. Feudalism was all but dead. Chivalry was dying. One could mock its conventions, as Jacques Coeur did in the sculptures of his great house in Bourges, where swineherds and shepherds mounted bareback on asses tilt with broomsticks, carrying basket lids for bucklers. Charles was indisputably the monarch of France.

We know well what Charles looked like, for Fouquet painted his likeness more than once, both from life and in death. When the King died in 1461, a cast of his face was rushed to Fouquet so that it might be painted *"comme au vif,"* according to the custom of the day. And then the artist turned to planning the decorations for the triumphal entry of the new king, Louis XI, who was to make Fouquet his royal artist, and to designing the sets for a mystery play that was to have accompanied the celebrations. His career was far from over, but during the preceding decade he had already completed the Book of Hours of Etienne Chevalier. Long ago the book was torn apart and its miniatures shorn of their surrounding embellishments. In its original state it was undoubtedly one of the most superb illuminated manuscripts of the late Middle Ages. What remains is enough to secure Fouquet's fame. Here he has reached an inimitable perfection. It has been called his "grand testament"; it is also a testament of the times.

These little parts of pages suggest the essence of Fouquet's art. In *The Adoration of the Magi* (see portfolio), with the candid realism that was so remarkable in his work, the artist cast his own royal patron, Charles VII, in the role of Melchior, humbly kneeling with his offering before the infant Christ. In violent contrast to this study of reverence and grace Fouquet has filled the background with a vivid scene of carnage and destruction. He was a consummate landscapist; and one could almost reconstruct the ancient monuments of Paris from the images of real buildings he has used in his settings. Into his depiction of Job, miserable on his dung heap and confronted by his three "comforters," Fouquet places the Château of Vincennes, rising majestically from such verdant fields as still surround Paris.

Italianisms abound in these illuminations, as we see so clearly in the architectural setting of *The Marriage of the Virgin* (although the building is prominently labeled "Solomon's temple") and in the foreground figure who breaks his barren rod against his knee—a figure straight from Italian Renaissance art. But there is purely northern realism in the other, fat-bellied creature who views the proceedings with such studiously feigned indifference. It was a prime aspect of Fouquet's genius that he could assimilate disparate influences from the early Florentines and contemporary Netherlanders and remain unquestionably master of his own art.

He was, as aforesaid, a man of his times. In *The Martyrdom of Saint Apollonia* (also reproduced in the portfolio) the gruesome ordeal of the tortured woman is presented against such a stage for a mystery play as Fouquet might have conceived for the royal celebrations a few years later. Everyone—spectators and participants (angels and devils alike) in their tiered boxes, torturers, the uncouth jester at the left, and the stage director at the right—everyone but the pitifully tried saint enjoys himself in this popular, communal medieval theater. In his *Pietà*, Fouquet again reminds us of his own age: France, like Christ, had known all the bitterness and weakness of a Passion, and when Fouquet used this image, his message was clear to his distinguished patron.

While the Middle Ages waned the preoccupation with death was profound, as the popularity of the *danses macabres* so poignantly witnessed. On virtually every surviving page of this Book of Hours, Fouquet emblazoned the name or initials of his patron the estimable Etienne Chevalier, ambassador and treasurer for two kings, a man of substance and proud of it. But the artist also included, as a point of reflection, a preview of the funeral of his living patron. In the end, he should be reminded, only the spirit mattered.

97

THEATER

Disturbing? Jean Genet is Downright Terrifying

At a time of sit-ins and freedom rides and Africa's astonishing birth of nations, it is almost inevitable that we should expect a play performed by Negroes, obsessed by ritual killings, and clanging with cries of hate and defiance, to offer some relevant comment on the race issue. Writing *The Blacks* in this era, Jean Genet has counted on our so reasoning.

The play is now being excellently performed in a production staged by Gene Frankel at the St. Marks Playhouse, off Broadway. But if you go to it in expectation of constructive discussion, ready to assist in proclaiming the long-deferred brotherhood of man, you may feel yourself cruelly rebuffed. People say glibly that Genet lives outside society, but they do not really consider what that implies. They continue to regard him as a rebel (i.e., a kind of violent reformer) and assume that, since he has undertaken a social theme, he must be moved by some impulse of goodwill, some wish to instruct or improve. But there is not a trace of goodwill in Genet, and the question of whether society is to be integrated or segregated is to him a matter of perfect indifference. It would still be society, and he would still be outside it.

It is in fact absurd, whatever the emphasis of the times, to expect this terrifying Frenchman to devote himself to civil rights, national aspirations, or in any way to produce a play of constructive social significance. What intimation has he ever given of such virtuous behavior? In his own life he has been a thief and a bawd (thrown out of five countries, tossed into thirteen jails before the age of thirty-five); in his plays he is an illusionist. As a youth he pursued a visionary absolute of degradation; the largely autobiographical *Our Lady of the Flowers* and *A Thief's Journal*, both written in jail, read for pages on end like the hallucinated ecstasies of an anti-saint. Both books, by the way, are scheduled for publication in America, an event that may finally break the back of our official censorship. The obscenity and scatology of these fictive memoirs are so perverse as to be numbing; the books are no more exciting—in the police sense of the word—than the fumes of ammonia are intoxicating.

It would be hazardous to guess what influences and experiences shaped this exuberant gymnast of evil. Criminals do not leave clear records, and Genet, naturally enough, is a liar. In *A Thief's Journal* he refers to himself as a foundling, and it may well be so, but I think he must have passed some of his earliest years outside public institutions. In *Our Lady of the Flowers*—also autobiographical, though more ambiguously so—there

is a little boy who lives with his widowed mother, a woman of fierce French respectability. He lives better than his fellows ("in the only house in the village, except for the church, that had a slate roof") and probably a good deal more gloomily—set apart and surrounded by gothic dreams: apparently he chews the leaves of aconite for the visions. A man corrupts this small child, and for this child corruption becomes a vision of the absolute. Similarly, the young Genet consecrated himself to wickedness with the fervor of a seminarian giving his life into the hands of the Almighty. But, alas for his vows, he was also an artist, and, in the end, he turned from the religion of vice to the aesthetics of subterfuge. "Metamorphosis lies in wait for us," he once wrote; also, "I am mad for fancy dress."

And metamorphosis in fancy dress is what he has been giving us ever since. "Disturbing" is, I believe, the adjective most commonly applied to Genet's plays. But he does not disturb so much by what he puts forward—in the manner, say, of Ibsen or Strindberg—as by the dislocation of expectation. His is the malaise of the missing stair tread, the question unanswered, the image that can be caught only as the eye blinks. Whatever is looked at straight-on in a Genet play disappears on the instant, or is

In The Blacks, *Jean Genet's startling exercise in multiple illusion and assault on his audience, several Negroes are masked to represent a white queen (right, center) and her retainers. Enthroned upstage, they serve as the mock counterpart of the audience they face out front, as they are entertained by a troupe of Negro players (opposite, downstage) who sardonically portray the seduction and murder of a white woman. (The woman, center, is played by a male in white mask.) At times the players at left step out of their roles to reveal their real selves and feelings.*

masters (those ranged on high, in their masks) have decided in advance to mete out to them. To heighten the effect, this play within a play is performed around a catafalque which, we are assured with much circumstantial detail, contains the body of the murdered white woman, transported hence in a Cadillac for the occasion.

Now it is clear that our Negro hosts cannot take this charade seriously, however hard they may try out of deference to our known prejudices. There is no body, there is no murder, and when the "whites" descend from their safe premises to administer justice in the "steaming jungle," it is they who expire, apparently by prearrangement: one of them has been heard, early in the evening, rehearsing his death speech. I take this detail to be a comment on the whites' understanding of the benevolent demise of colonialism.

At the same time, it is also clear that this inept drama—the performers who are vivid "out of character" become wooden as "actors"—is introduced not only to entertain us but to divert us from what is taking place elsewhere. And that is the off-stage play within a play. A messenger named Edgar Alas Newport News (the names in the play are all wicked parodies of the white man's concept of Negro nomenclature—Felicity Trollop Pardon, Adelaide Bobo, etc.) keeps running in with word of a trial. A traitor has been caught, there are cryptic asides about the Negro learning to take responsibility for his own justice, eyes are rolled at the audience, there is a good deal of shushing. Then, as the on-stage play is approaching its climax in the jungle, word comes that justice has been carried out. All crowd around the messenger, who affirms that it is so and adds that "another" has been appointed in "his" place and is "on his way." The masks are forgotten, various people start to wander off, remarking that they have jobs to do. But then they bethink themselves of the audience sitting there all agog and decide that the flummery had better be carried out to the end: "as we could not allow the Whites to be present at a deliberation . . . that does not concern them, and as, in order to cover up, we have had to fabricate the only one that does concern them."

It is at this point that Genet's trap is set to snap. When someone throws up a screen, we believe instinctively that it is designed to hide something. And when we penetrate a subterfuge, we believe in-

101

stinctively that what we have come upon is real. It is not easy to remember that Genet is a liar. But our hosts have told us several times that they are performing not what they are but what we believe them to be. How then do they describe this off-stage "other" who is "going off to organize and continue the fight"? "Just as you would imagine him," says Newport News, smiling. "Exactly as he must be in order to spread panic by force and cunning." What about his voice, someone asks. "It's deep. Somewhat caressing. He'll first have to fascinate and then convince. Yes, he's also a charmer."

And he's also a figment of generalizations and clichés—just as the audience would imagine him. The trick behind the trick is obvious enough, set down so; but by the time *The Blacks* gets to these lines, the audience is feeling as white as bone. It has been made to feel excluded by its color (a rare sensation for whites); it suspects that baubles have been danced before its eyes to obscure the real affairs of life. So now it hears in those empty words of Newport News a charming menace, and its hair stirs along the spine. Being very much on edge, made acutely conscious that "we" are not "they," it is not quick to notice that one of the girls asks, "But . . . at least he's black?" At that everyone laughs. You bet he's black—indeed, that's all he is, a blackness in the white man's blood.

Of course, we would recover ourselves in a moment, but before we can, the minuet resumes and we are smilingly dismissed. Thus Genet puts to the test the vaunted tolerance and humane flexibility of contemporary society. "All men are brothers" is our fervent carol, but how well does it stand up to a little insolence, a little exclusion, some enigmatic mumbo jumbo? It is humiliating to find one's façade of goodwill so thin.

At the end of the play one has a most curious sensation while going through the conventional courtesies: the bows of the performers seem insulting; the applause of the audience sounds defensive, there is no cordiality about it—we were told we could be had, and we were had. Because, as it turns out, we too can have our color used against us.

Genet is now quite the lion of the Paris salons, and I'm told that hostesses are wont to put a piece of silver, or some charming bric-a-brac, temptingly within his reach: there is always the chance of enjoying the glory of being robbed by so distinguished a guest. Such a man must have a particular understanding of what it means to let bygones be bygones. For he too is one of the blacks—one of those on whom we others have sat in judgment. It is remarkable how clean of heart one must be to come safely within the spell of this black and unrepentant sinner.   ROBERT HATCH

RADIO

O for the Days of Amos 'n' Andy!

During the last few months I have been doing a great deal of driving through a great deal of dull countryside, and as a consequence I have renewed my acquaintance with radio—old-fashioned, low-fidelity AM radio, like mother used to make. Radio and I got along quite well together over a good many years, but we had a falling-out over Tony Wons and have since gone our separate ways. After this recent exposure to what passes for radio today, I can only remark that the chances for a reconciliation are not good.

Actually the breakup was never absolute, for family reasons. During the winter, every time it snows my wife gets an eye open early in the morning and tunes in to the no-school notices; the children scramble into the room and stand by breathlessly to learn whether they have come out the winner in this particular storm, or whether they will be forced once again to beat their rugged way to school in their primitive, plush-lined, heated school bus. As soon as this vital matter is disposed of, the radio gets switched to FM and stays there until the next storm. FM radio doesn't give no-school notices in the morning; just I Musici playing Corelli.

I never gave this much thought. I presumed it was a noble service performed by radio for the weary housewife in all states except those like Arizona, which doesn't have snow, and Virginia, which doesn't have schools. It never occurred to me that the no-school notices, far from being brief interludes in an otherwise busy day, were actually the high point of the schedule, and that from the no-school notice on, it was downhill all the way.

It has all become so distressingly trivial. Worst of all, the stations I am referring to are still trying. Most AM stations have long since given up and now do nothing from dawn to dawn but play phonograph records of rock-and-roll. I suppose it is rock-and-roll, but I don't keep very well in touch with the teen-age mob, and for all I know there's another name for it now. Anyway, the records haven't changed and neither have the hysterical announcers, and I think that disposes of the subject. Although a casual sweep over the dial may not reveal it, there are a great many stations which do *not* broadcast rock-and-roll. Unfortunately, except for the very rare big-city stations, like WQXR and WNYC in New York, what they do broadcast is really not much better.

It's still records—all the Perry Como you could possibly want to hear, intermixed with Frank Sinatra, Rosemary Clooney, and other estimable pop singers. Revenue comes from the local merchant, together with those indefatigable national advertisers, the cigarette companies and the toothpaste companies. (Cigarettes put the stain on, toothpaste takes it off, and the American economy marches inexorably forward.) Separating the entertainers and the hucksters are the no-school notices, or their equivalent, which go on all day. I am now in a position to march directly to the regular meeting of the St. Mary's Women's Sodality in eighty-four different communities. I know where the P.T.A. meets, and when it meets, and why it meets, for all towns on the Eastern seaboard from Caribou, Maine, to Naples, Florida.

I find this all rather saddening. Radio's lifetime and my own have always seemed to me to be running in parallel. We were invented, big-time radio and small-time I, at about the same time. We passed through infancy together. We had our troubles during adolescence: the government forced NBC to divest itself of one of its networks, and my father wouldn't let me have a car. We both came of age during the thirties. After that came a time when radio, I must admit, was doing a great deal better than I, but it has declined rapidly, and we are now falling into the sere and yellow leaf together.

The advertising journals tell me that more people are listening to radio than ever before in history, and fling statistics about to prove the point. I always study the tabulations with great care, simply because of my personal involvement; I cannot escape the impression that anything said about radio is also being said about me. The statistics bear me out, for more people than ever are listening to me, too, but no one seems to be paying any attention. And that is exactly the way it is with radio.

Remember what it was once upon a time? During the heyday of Amos 'n' Andy the fifteen minutes between 7 and 7:15 were sacrosanct. No effort was spared to keep them so, to the extent that the city of Detroit once reported that more toilets were flushed directly after 7:15 than at any other period during the day or night—so many more, in fact, that the water system lacked resources to keep up with the demand and fish were floundering on the banks of the Detroit River. Analysts of the state of the arts were never able to make up their minds exactly what this meant, but it had to mean something. I myself, cruising in leisurely fashion down Long Island Sound on the old Fall River Line, once narrowly escaped death from capsizing, when the entire ship's complement—crew, passengers, and scarlet ladies—raced simultaneously to the port side at 7 P.M. sharp to gather around the vessel's sole radio set and learn what the Kingfish would be up to next. I like to think it was my lonely presence at starboard that pulled the ship through.

It seems odd that in a few brief years radio should have gone so thoroughly to seed. It was called a triumph of the communications arts, an amazing instrument of news and entertainment and information, one of mankind's greatest weapons against ignorance and isolation. And it was every one of those things—it still is. But it has descended to the raucous and the trivial, shouldered out of the way entirely by the monster television.

Yet it has great advantages over television, and it accomplished much that television hasn't yet approached. No one will forget the superb jobs that Elmer Davis and Raymond Swing and Edward R. Murrow used to do, day in and day out, in giving dimension to the news and bringing intelligent minds to bear upon its significance. Television, which seems to be damned with an inherent requirement for gimmickry, cannot do anything as straightforward as that. Even today news on radio is still news and not a few sentences to go with the pictures someone found lying around the studio. Laughter on radio was laughter, and even when it came in response to a cue card, it came from the throats of real people and not from a magnetic tape. (Let me pause in passing to remark upon a phenomenon. Humorists in radio once worked in studios and complained because they thought they needed live audiences; Will Rogers, I seem to remember, was the first to insist and the first to win the point. With television, humorists began to complain that audiences didn't laugh heartily enough, or at the right places, and they have now gone back to studios. Humorists are difficult people.)

I suspect that once again we can look to the unfortunate marriage between advertising and radio for the source of the trouble. The way the contract was drawn, with the advertiser in almost total control, it was inevitable that support would be withdrawn from radio the moment television began to command the bigger, and the more easily befuddled, audience. There is no reason at all why radio should not be able to provide first-rate dramatic entertainment, and comedy, and news, and comment upon the news—no reason except money, and the money simply isn't there.

Attention is suddenly being directed toward the vast wasteland of television —and it is vast, and it is a wasteland— but except for a few stations in a few large cities, there is a vast wasteland of radio that not even the FCC seems to care very much about. More's the pity. Given half the chance, I could like radio.

STEPHEN WHITE

103

BOOKS

Henry Miller's Stream of Self-consciousness

When you first read Henry Miller's *Tropic of Cancer,* you are apt to conclude that it was written during a series of lengthy drinking bouts.

> *Could man be drunk for ever*
> *With liquor, love, or fights,*
> *Lief should I rouse at morning*
> *And lief lie down of nights.*

So wrote A. E. Housman, concluding sadly that it was impossible: "men at whiles are sober and think by fits and starts." But Henry Miller at first seems to have mastered this impossibility, and to differ from ordinary men as a perpetual drunkard from an abstainer. Occasionally in the lounge car of a train, while you are peacefully reading, someone who has had too many highballs bumps his fat behind into the chair beside you and begins telling you a long incoherent story about this girl in the office, name's Dolores, and what the poor broad said to the floor manager, wasn't her fault anyhow, never saw such a lousy deal, reminds me of a time once out in Seattle when the salesmen all got stoned at the Christmas party, should have seen them, boy, never forget it. Waiter, let's have another here, sure you won't? I still got forty minutes, but as I was saying this stinking brother-in-law of mine. . . .

Much of Miller's writing reads something like that: an endless gush of reminiscence about people who are never introduced to the reader and are sometimes hardly credible. Some of them appear and are drawn in vivid detail, then vanish forever. Others fly into the story and out again, like a bat through a garage. Neither *Tropic of Cancer* nor its sequel *Tropic of Capricorn* is a novel in any ordinary sense: that is, a story with a coherent plot developed in time and a cast of characters interacting on one another. They are sections of a non-stop monologue.

Basically this monologue is like the gabble of the drunkard on the train—with two important exceptions. One is that its style is marvelous. The other is that its subject matter rises far higher than that of the average monologist and sinks far lower. Much of it consists of rhapsodic prose poems on Life, and Art, and Individuality, and the horrors of the Modern World, and so forth. Much of it is conversation so filthy that it is never heard outside prisons, barrack rooms, and the lowest slums—together with vivid narratives of mean and degrading actions. It is often very funny, at least to men. Taken as a whole it makes you detest and despise Henry Miller. You try to pity him, but you simply cannot. Not at first; perhaps not ever.

Open *Tropic of Cancer* at its first page:

I am living at the Villa Borghese. There is not a crumb of dirt anywhere, not a chair misplaced. We are all alone here and we are dead.

Last night Boris discovered that he was lousy. I had to shave his armpits and even then the itching did not stop.

This makes very little sense. How in twenty devils' name can Henry Miller be living with a single companion at the Villa Borghese? It is a beautiful place, of course, but it is the property of the Republic of Italy, it is full of superb paintings and lamentable tourists, and it is carefully controlled by the Department of Fine Arts. (From Alfred Perlès's book *My Friend Henry Miller* we learn that Villa Borghese was Miller's comic disguise name for a real place in Paris called the Villa Seurat; but who is to know this right off the bat?) And how can the two men be dead, if one is verminous? Body vermin always leave a corpse. All right, it is a hyperbole: they are lonely and clean, therefore dead, like well-washed cadavers. Then how, in all this cleanliness, does one of them acquire lice? And, curiouser and curiouser, why does the other have to shave the pediculous man's armpits? Is Boris paralyzed, so that he cannot shave his own armpits? The operation presents few technical difficulties. Or does Henry like telling us in the opening paragraphs of his book that he was so degraded, living on another man's charity, that he was compelled as part of his duties as a dependent to shave the armpits of his host? It would be like the clients whom Juvenal describes as holding the chamber pot in the dining room while their rich patron relieved himself: a peaceful though unappetizing symbiosis. But why does he stop there? Perhaps he is squeamish?

No. As we read on in *Tropic of Cancer,* we realize that Henry is not squeamish. He may not be logical, but he is immune from the etiolating vice of fastidiousness. Perhaps on this first page he wishes to leave something to the reader's imagination. Later, he makes no such concessions.

But having read these first sentences of *Tropic of Cancer,* you will remember them. Henry Miller can use the language. He writes strong, biting, memorable, vivid prose. Often it is unjust to begin criticizing a book by taking out its first few sentences. But Henry Miller is a rhetorician: he knows that the exordium is important. His books and his chapters begin dramatically, pungently. Style, style, style: brushwork, the drive of the hand into the clay, the thrust of the lines of structure against each other, the movement of the musical phrase between keys and modes, the balance and rivalry of colors, the rise and fall and timing of an actor's voice —style is a chief aim of all artists in all media. This Henry Miller has achieved: he is a wonderful stylist.

Spontaneous, his style appears. He writes prose which often seems to run absolutely naturally, like the flow of eager conversation or a rapidly written letter or the current of nonlogical ideas in one's own mind. If in the future he is remembered for anything more than his interest in obscenity, he will be recalled as an agile, often graceful, sometimes powerful manipulator of word and phrase and sentence and paragraph, and sometimes (although less often) of those larger units which are called chapters. He seems to be talking to you as you read him. He can even get away with old-fashioned tricks such as the address (half-ironical, no doubt) "Dear reader." It is easy to believe that he is an enthusiastic letter writer and has poured out tens of thousands of pages of correspondence to his friends. (Much of it has been preserved, and will no doubt in time be acquired by Yale, although I wonder whether it will be published.) Writing even one letter a day is practice for a writer, provided it is not formal or commercial but intimate and friendly. Writing as many letters as Miller does is like a violinist's playing three hours of exercises every morning.

Some of his most ardent admirers are professional writers: Lawrence Durrell, Karl Shapiro, and others. They themselves have struggled with the Laocoön serpent of language, trying to master it before it inwound and paralyzed them, and they delight in Miller's superb conquest of it. Even one of his short works such as *The Air-Conditioned Nightmare* makes your heart beat faster and your brain move more quickly, if you like language. Stylistically, compared with most regular novels, *Tropic of Cancer* and *Tropic of Capricorn* are like two big symphonies for eighty-piece orchestras contrasted with two chamber works by Karl Ditters von Dittersdorf.

True, he rambles a great deal. Frequently, especially in *Capricorn*, he goes off into illogical rhapsodies which remind us partly of Thomas Wolfe's barbaric yawp and partly of those Dadaist and surrealistic prose poems which nowadays seem something of a waste of printer's ink. But he has mastered the art of rhetoric. Open either *Tropic* at random, and begin to read. The only reason you will stop is that you are either exhausted or nauseated. Before writing this paragraph, I let *Capricorn* fall open. Page 256: "I remember Sunday mornings in the little old house near the cemetery. I remember sitting at the piano in my nightshirt, working away at the pedals with bare feet, and the folks lying in bed toasting themselves in the next room. . . ." and off he goes into four grand continuous pages about music and Wittgenstein and Prokofiev and a scherzo Henry improvised to a louse discovered in his underwear—a real bravura piece of writing impossible to interrupt or ignore. And it modulates straight into a piece of narrative about his first sexual experience, with his music teacher, which both in language and in content is revolting. And yet it is written with the same driving energy, the same rich variety of phrasing, the same lively offbeat sentence structure, the same admirable spontaneity, the same crazy humor.

This is the paradox of Henry Miller. The two *Tropics* are among the foulest books ever written. *Cancer* is bad enough, but *Capricorn* gets worse as it goes on and reaches depths of vileness which are really indescribable. Miller's obscenity is not like Lawrence's obscenity in *Lady Chatterley's Lover,* which was meant to be "natural," unaffected, and inspiring. It is closer to the astounding obscenity of Rabelais and Aristophanes, but it is far less wholesome. Some obscenity is normal. Much of Miller's is abnormal: the kind of thing that goes on only among the lowest.

Why did Miller write it? Why, for instance, did he trouble to describe himself as going with a miserable prostitute and then stealing the wage he had given her? He has genius. Why does he want to show himself as a swine? He gives several answers to this: the customary flapdoodle about the Artist being a separate species of humanity with unique privileges, the bold assertion that the entire world is all wrong and the sooner it is blown up the better, the adolescent notion that sex alone "holds the world together," and so on. The line between genius and derangement is often hard to draw, and the literary evidence suggests that he was close to the latter when he wrote these books. When Jung read James Joyce's *Ulysses* he said, "Good; if he hadn't written this he would have gone mad." It seems that the two *Tropics* represent two different stages in Miller's abnormality. When they were written he was one of a group which we are, in this curious era, beginning to find more and more fascinating, the crazy artists.

And what drove him into this condition? You will not find the explanation in *Tropic of Cancer:* it contains only a description of the middle stages of the malady. The explanation lies in *Capricorn*. Although there were several convergent causes, the strongest is hinted at within the final thirty pages, as though (consciously or unconsciously) he had held it back to the very end. It is in a hideous waking dream of his adolescent years.

I seemed to have absolute liberty and the authority of a god, and yet by some capricious turn of events the end would be that I'd be lying on the sacrificial block and one of my charming uterine relatives would be bending over me with a gleaming knife to cut out my heart.

Miller says he had two "uterine relatives." One was an idiot sister, whom his mother used to beat savagely. The other was his mother. Whose face did he see bending over him with the knife?

GILBERT HIGHET

105

By H. R. TREVOR-ROPER

THE TWO SPAINS OF DON QUIXOTE

The only good book in Spanish literature, said Montesquieu, is the one which proves all the others bad. He was referring, of course, to that incomparable, irresistible, unique work, *Don Quixote*, whose first part was published in 1605, and which, it is said, killed by ridicule the "romances of chivalry" that had been the staple literary diet of Spaniards for a century. Certainly they did not survive it. The most famous, most persistent of them all, *Amadis de Gaul*, was last reissued in 1602, three years before *Don Quixote* appeared; and thereafter, in America as in Spain, the whole literary genus was practically extinct. But whether *Don Quixote* really killed them, or merely appeared as their epitaph, is a difficult question, a question to be solved, if at all, rather in the field of social than of literary history. In this essay I wish to consider the social background to Don Quixote and seek in it, if possible, the key to its unique quality and marvelous success.

Of course no masterpiece is completely explained by circumstances. By definition, a masterpiece proceeds from the human genius of its author, not from the material which he uses. But it is undeniable that Cervantes, though his work has transcended the age which it described, was—perhaps more than any other great writer—a child of his time. No other of his works has gained immortality. Only in this did his happy spirit attain perfection. And even in this he showed himself essentially a recorder, not (like Dickens or Tolstoy) a critic or reformer of his own age. A great Hispanist, A. Morel-Fatio, has called *Don Quixote* "the great social novel of early seventeenth-century Spain"; but he has added, "No writer has been more of his time than Cervantes;

he is not ahead of it by one line." Therefore, in considering its character, we are justified in looking carefully at the material out of which it was made: the personal experience of Cervantes in sixteenth-century Spain.

First of all, what is the essential quality of *Don Quixote?* The plot of the book is soon told. Don Quixote is a middle-aged Castilian hidalgo—that is, a poor but proud rustic gentleman—who for many years has lived in his decrepit manor house in La Mancha, a seedy, remote province of Spain, alone with his niece and his old housekeeper, reading "romances of chivalry." Of these romances of chivalry we shall have something to say in a moment: at present it is enough to say that the constant reading of them has, by the beginning of the story, unhinged Don Quixote's mind, and so he sets out, with his equally decrepit and equally engaging horse Rozinante, in order that he too may seek similar adventures, opposing giants, rescuing damsels from dragons and enchanters, and challenging rival knights-errant to single combat to prove the superior beauty of their respective ladies. For such a purpose Don Quixote needs a lady, and so he idealizes, as the Lady Dulcinea del Toboso, a local farmer's daughter. He also, like all knights-errant, needs a trusty squire. For this function he impresses a devoted but hardheaded, earth-bound local peasant, the perfect foil to his own high, chivalric fantasies, Sancho Panza.

Once the dramatis personae are assembled, the action seems almost automatic. Don Quixote and Sancho Panza set out: the former boldly, with all his bees buzzing in his exalted bonnet, and the latter reluctantly, awed by his master's high language, but thinking primarily of incidental

This portrait of Miguel de Cervantes (attributed to Juan de Jaure-
gui) shows the proudly Spanish
and idealistic mien of a man who
might have been Don Quixote himself—as indeed Cervantes to some
extent was. His early life was spent
in the service of a Roman cardinal,
in military action, and—five years
of it—in an Algerian prison. It was
in another jail, much later, that he
conceived the idea of Don Quixote.

cakes and ale and ultimate material reward. To Don Quixote
the real world hardly exists. To him inns are castles, inn-
keepers their constables, windmills giants, flocks of sheep
rival armies, funeral processions troops of enchanters carrying off their spellbound victims; and whenever these ma-
jestic misconceptions painfully conflict with the real world,
he explains the real world away with yet more ingenious
rationalizations. But to Sancho Panza, though he takes his
master's theories on trust, there is ultimately only one real
world, and that is the world which he has left behind in his
village, exchanging it not for ideal adventures but, as he
discovers, for solid bumps and bruises, the price to him of
his master's chivalry.

Don Quixote and Sancho Panza are inseparable: they are
the joint heroes of the book, and the book owes its character
to this constant duality. But it is not a crude duality. It may
begin as such, but little by little, as we read on, we find that
it becomes increasingly subtle. For the contrast is not really
between the knight and his squire, it is *in* them both. Don
Quixote may be mad when conversation is of knights and
ladies, dwarfs and enchanters, but in other matters he has
remarkable good sense, which breaks disconcertingly through
his follies. Sancho Panza may be, at bottom, a hardheaded,
prosaic peasant, but periodically he too is carried away into
the world of fantasy, fitting himself into his master's world
and imagining himself rewarded with the government of an
island. To the firm overtones there are always subtle under-
tones: the whole world of Cervantes is schizophrenic, and
the men in his novel merely participate, in differing degrees,
in both the reality and the make-believe.

Consider their attitude toward the books of chivalry, the
clearly convicted source of all the make-believe. At first it
seems that Don Quixote alone takes seriously what other
men regard merely as foolish novelettes. But soon we realize
that this is not so. Everyone may agree that these "lying
histories" are pernicious works which have made the poor
knight mad; but everyone, it transpires, is as deep in them
as he, and perhaps just as affected by them, though in other
ways. When Don Quixote has set off on his adventures, there
is dismay in his home, and his housekeeper and his niece,
together with the barber and the curate, as pillars of sanity,
resolve to burn all the wicked books that have disordered
his mind. But what is the result? As each book is identified,
they all remember it, discuss its merits, argue about its fate;
and half of them are ultimately saved from the burning.

Later, when the same barber and curate pursue Don
Quixote to the inn in the Sierra Morena, which is the theater
of his follies, they explain to the innkeeper the origin of his
madness, only to discover that the innkeeper, his housekeeper, his daughter, and his maid are all passionate readers
of such romances: How then, they exclaim, can such delightful reading, which keeps them alive, make anyone mad?
Later still, when the curate and the barber bring Don
Quixote back to his village in a cage on an oxcart—a won-
derfully comic episode—they are overtaken by a canon of
the Church, whom Don Quixote gravely informs that he has
been bewitched and encaged by jealous enchanters. Having
then heard the true story from his escort, the canon ex-
presses indignation against those pernicious books which the
Church has constantly but ineffectively condemned. But as

Below: Under Charles V (at left in this double portrait by Antonio Arias) Spain grew into a great world power; but under his son, Philip II (at right), the momentum slackened and ruinous wars left Spain drained and disillusioned. Right: Cervantes, a hero before he was a writer, lost the use of his left hand in action against the Turks at Lepanto in 1571. This engraving, made at some later date, shows him in the thick of the fight (center) with his hand bandaged.

UNIVERSITY OF GRANADA, SPAIN

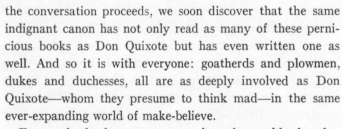

the conversation proceeds, we soon discover that the same indignant canon has not only read as many of these pernicious books as Don Quixote but has even written one as well. And so it is with everyone: goatherds and plowmen, dukes and duchesses, all are as deeply involved as Don Quixote—whom they presume to think mad—in the same ever-expanding world of make-believe.

For as the book progresses, so does the world of make-believe. The barber and the curate, who set out to cure Don Quixote's follies, end by becoming participants in it, actors in his imaginary history. Sancho Panza starts talking his master's language. The Duke and Duchess, who receive the pair, adjust their whole dukedom to his follies, so that Don Quixote is no longer any madder than his surroundings, and Sancho, with perfect gravity, gives laws to his imaginary island. Well might a bystander cry out, on seeing our hero, "The Devil take thee for Don Quixote of La Mancha! Thou art a madman; and wert thou so in private, 'twere less evil; but thy property is to make all that converse or treat with thee madmen and coxcombs!" Finally, by an exquisite piece of fancy, Don Quixote himself becomes the champion of truth against falsehood. For in 1614, nine years after its publication, the success of Cervantes's first part had prompted a rival novelist to publish a continuation of the story. Cervantes was indignant at this plagiarism, and in his own second part, which appeared the following year, he showed Don Quixote, now made famous by the first part, continually meeting and confuting the misguided readers of "the false second part." Thus the genuine first part and the false second part of the story become additional elements

in its last phase, complicating still further the delicious and now inextricable confusion of reality and make-believe.

Such, very briefly, is the character of this incomparable work. I have described it as a "schizophrenic" book because of the duality of heroism and disillusion, make-believe and reality, which so completely pervades it. It is this duality which makes the book, sustaining and animating it throughout its great length—indeed, so animating it that Dr. Johnson could describe it as the only book which one wishes were longer. And it does so because the duality is genuine. Cervantes himself, we feel, is schizophrenic; he is on both sides at once: on the side of Don Quixote and on the side of Sancho Panza. The duality, in fact, is in his own mind, and —since he is so completely "of his time"—in the society in which he lived, late sixteenth- and early seventeenth-century Spain.

In what sense was Spain, in those years, schizophrenic? If we look at it closely, I believe we can find an answer. In Cervantes's lifetime, Spain had two very different moods. They were the moods of two successive but antithetical generations. The generation of the fathers was bound together by one set of experiences which created one kind of mood, a mood of fantastic confidence, heroic tension, intoxicating romance. The generation of the sons had different experiences, and consequently a different mood. Immune from their fathers' experiences, they knew only defeat, disappointment, disillusion; and their mood was one of cynical realism, passivity, emptiness. Now the life of Cervantes straddled both these generations, and in his own person he experienced, directly, both the heroism of the fathers and the

FROM *Vida de Miguel de Cervantes Saavedra,* J. MORAN, MADRID 1863

One of the eight known copies of the first edition of Don Quixote *(title page at left) recently brought $44,000 at a New York auction. The first illustrations of Sancho Panza and the Don appeared in the English edition of 1620 (right).*

disillusion of the sons. In his book, which is in some ways an autobiography, or at least a self-portrait, he expressed—sympathetically, because he had felt them both—the two mutually opposing moods, moods which met in his lifetime and, particularly, in him.

Let us look at these two generations, so close in time, so opposite in character. First, let us take the generation of the fathers, the men who grew up during the reign of Charles V, "the Emperor"; for he was Holy Roman Emperor while king of Spain. Under the Emperor, Spain found itself suddenly a world power. Not long before, it had been a poor, rural appendix at the back end of Europe; now its armies fought and conquered on the Rhine and the Danube, in Italy and Africa, against German heretics and Turkish infidels. Spanish adventurers were conquering huge empires (and huge estates for themselves) in new-found America; and the wealth of America, spent on armies, fleets, and the imperial court, sustained and inflated an archaic feudal society, with chivalric notions imported from the magnificent Burgundy of Froissart and Comines.

It was an astonishing change, astonishing in its suddenness, comparable with the great Arab conquests of the seventh and eighth centuries; and the Spaniards who witnessed or achieved it were inspired by a sense of divine mission and superhuman power. God was behind them, they felt, and nothing beyond them. They flinched before no obstacle, accepted no authority except that of their own king. Even the Pope received scant respect from them: when he was tiresome, the imperial court, inspired by the exciting, liberal doctrines of Erasmus, did not hesitate to strike at

him, and the imperial armies seized and sacked the Holy City itself. Only the Emperor himself commanded unconditional respect; and he commanded it the more because, from a foreigner, a Fleming who knew no Spanish, he had become a Spaniard: *"esta figura tan española!"* ("this truly Spanish figure!") as a great historian has called him, who refused, even to the Pope's ambassador, to speak any language but the Spanish which he had lately learned.

It was this mood of exaltation in the time of the Emperor which found its popular expression in the famous "romances of chivalry." Throughout the sixteenth century, but particularly in the Emperor's reign, they were the best sellers of Spain, the equivalent of our "science fiction"; for though absurd in content, they symbolized a boundless new confidence which found nothing impossible. The adventures of Amadis de Gaul, Policisne de Boecia, Palmerin de Oliva, and their descendants were published and republished in serial form—scholars have counted 316 editions in the sixteenth century—and there is scarcely a famous Spaniard of "the golden century" who was not an avowed or secret reader of them: for the condemnation of the Church was powerless to suppress them. Wounded at Pamplona, the young Ignatius of Loyola spent his convalescence reading them, and when he became a missionary saint, his activities read like one of them: he became a knight-errant of religion. Saint Teresa of Avila confesses that in her youth she was never happy unless she was secretly reading them.

The Emperor himself, ignoring the protests of his clergy, was a constant reader and even wrote a sequel to one of them. They were the favorite reading of his soldiers in Italy.

109

Few subjects have inspired as many artists as Don Quixote and Sancho Panza. In the nineteenth century Gustave Doré applied his operatic style to the Don's disastrous tilt with the windmills (left). Goya satirized the hero as mordantly as Cervantes himself, showing him (right) deluded by chivalric tales, beset by all the demons of the wicked world, championing fair damsels. And one of the most memorable images is Daumier's gaunt knight on his shambling horse, trailed by Sancho on his donkey (opposite).

In spite of an official ban they poured into the Indies. When the companions of Cortes looked for the first time on the lake of Mexico, studded with Aztec cities, "we were amazed," says one of them, "and said that it was like the enchanted things related in the book of Amadis de Gaul." The passion of the Spanish soldiers in America for these "lying histories" has left its traces today: California in the Northern Hemisphere, Patagonia in the Southern, are both named after heroines of these trashy novelettes.

Charles V abdicated the Spanish throne in 1556, retiring (with two books of chivalry in his luggage) to the monastery of Yuste, and three years later his son and successor, Philip II, came to Spain. Later historians have seen Philip II as a great ruler, but it is worth noting that this respect for the uniformly unsuccessful bureaucrat-king did not begin until the reign of his grandson, when few could remember him. To contemporaries he was a poor figure, mean, jealous, and suspicious. In his reign the old liberalism of Charles V was finally crushed, the last of the old "Erasmians" burnt; the Empire was frayed at its edges and rotted at its core. But this decline was not at first apparent. For a decade, at least, after 1560, the heirs of Charles V kept his spirit alive. Particularly it lived on in Italy, away from the stuffy bigotry and waspish intrigues of the new court. There all eyes looked south and east to the great crusade which Charles V had conducted from Italy, the defense of the Mediterranean against the Turk. In 1571 the dead Emperor seemed to live again when his bastard son, Don John of Austria, of whom his legitimate son was so jealous, won a resounding naval victory at Lepanto (for which the church bells were rung even in Protestant England) and went on to occupy Tunis, ending forever the Turkish domination of the Mediterranean.

But if Lepanto echoed the imperial age, it was the last echo. In the 1570's Don John was undermined by his royal brother and died, and meanwhile Spain itself was being slowly ruined by a gigantic, ill-conceived, desk-dictated policy of religious and political reaction in northern Europe. By 1590 the new generation had grown up: a generation with no memory of the imperial days and their buoyant mood. Instead it had experienced only disillusion and defeat. For the last twenty years it had seen Spain mobilizing massive efforts which only disintegrated in humiliating disaster and squalid recrimination. All the wealth of America had been poured out in vain. The long revolt in the Netherlands was still unquenched. The Invincible Armada had been shattered. The attempt to conquer France had failed. In the years that followed, the disasters pressed nearer home. In the 1590's there was both plague and famine in Spain. The Crown was bankrupt, the nation impoverished. The political and military scandals were great and public. In 1596 an English force, under Queen Elizabeth's Earl of Essex, actually landed in Spain and seized and sacked its greatest port, Cádiz. Two years later, after a long and terrible illness, as slow and agonizing as his reign, Philip II died, and with his son, Philip III, was enthroned the new spirit of Spain—the spirit of cynicism and disillusion, the negation of all heroism, the cult not of religious crusades but of passive, superstitious piety.

The contrast between the new spirit and the old is re-

markable. Wherever we look, it is there. In politics a wooden defensiveness replaces adventure; in literature satire replaces bombast. Social values are different: the old aristocracy had been military leaders; the new give themselves up to the giddy pursuit of official status and expensive pleasure. And religion reflects the same change. In the sixteenth century the Spanish Church had been active, crusading, missionary: its heroes had been Las Casas, Loyola, Saint Teresa; in the seventeenth, it is dull and passive: its only great figure is Molinos, the founder, appropriately, of religious quietism.

Perhaps the most striking illustration of this new spirit is the sudden change which took place, early in the seventeenth century, in the patron saint of Spain. For centuries that saint had been *Santiago*—Saint James, who was reputed to have come to Spain, and who was there transformed into a fighting saint, the patron of holy war. He was known as *Santiago Matamoros*, "Santiago, the killer of Moors." All through the Middle Ages, Santiago inspired Spanish Christians fighting against the infidel. Again and again, in the critical moment of battles, he appeared to them, mounted on a white horse in the sky, to give them fresh courage and turn defeat into victory. In America, too, fighting far from home against overwhelming odds, the conquistadors often saw Santiago, sometimes alone on his white horse, sometimes at the head of an ethereal army, doing battle for them in the clouds. More than two hundred places in Latin America still commemorate his name. But then, quite suddenly, in Spain and America alike, his authenticity was challenged. The doubters—Cervantes himself among them—raised their

voices; there was a brief struggle, conducted in full legal form; and in 1617, Santiago, the saint of crusade and victory, collapsed. He was replaced, in Spain, by Saint Teresa of Avila—or rather by an imaginary Saint Teresa, not the real saint, that "gadabout nun," social, energetic, practical; but a gaping *beata*, as we see her in Bernini's effigy, the personification of passive, inexhaustible female credulity. In America, having appeared at least ten times in the sixteenth century, Santiago showed himself only once in the seventeenth and then disappeared. He was replaced in Mexico by the creole San Felipe de Jesús, in Peru by another female *beata*, the half-caste Santa Rosa de Lima. This sudden change of saints symbolizes a change in the whole religious character of Spain.

I have dwelt upon this sudden shift, in one generation of Spanish life, from heroic tension to empty disillusion, because it was the essential background to Cervantes's own life, the background to *Don Quixote*. Cervantes, in a sense, fell between the two generations, sharing the moods of both. Born in 1547, in the reign of Charles V, he was brought up in Spain by an old Erasmian teacher who still breathed the confident, liberal air of imperial times; and then, as a young man, he went to Italy and was intoxicated by the ebullience, the vitality of Italian life. He read Ariosto, the poet of gaiety, chivalry, and enchanted romance. He enlisted as a soldier, fought and lost his left hand in Don John's great, victorious battle of Lepanto, served in the campaign against Tunis and Goletta, and in 1575 set sail, full of honor and pride, and with letters of recommendation from Don John and the Spanish governor in his pocket, for Spain, promo-

111

By the twentieth century Don Quixote had traveled around the world. In Japan, Quixote-san—wearing full samurai regalia—braves a tigerish lion in its den (below), as his onlookers tremble. And behind the Iron Curtain, Don Quixote becomes the symbol of oppressed idealism pitted against the decadent aristocracy—although in this Czech illustration he is only studying his "woeful countenance" (right).

FROM *Pribehy Dona Quijota*, ORBIS, PRAGUE 1946

KEISUKE SERIZAWA

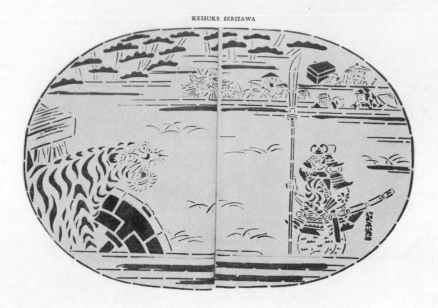

tion, and further glory. He was a hero, a self-conscious hero, living fully and investing heavily in that (as he was to discover) last twilight of the heroic age. Nor did his heroism end there. On his way home, off the coast of France, his ship was captured by Algerian corsairs. Seeing his letters of recommendation, the pirates presumed him to be a man of mark who would command a high ransom. Cervantes was taken to Algiers and there remained for more than five years, a prisoner and a galley slave.

In his captivity at Algiers, Cervantes continued his heroic exploits. He never forgot them. Long afterward, in *Don Quixote,* he recalled them. There, a captive, escaped from the Moorish galleys, meets Don Quixote and tells the story of his captivity. In it he refers to a fellow captive "called something-de-Saavedra" (Cervantes's full name was Miguel de Cervantes Saavedra), who achieved such a personal ascendancy over the Moorish governor that although "we all feared that he should be broached on the stake for the least of many things he did . . . yet he never struck him nor commanded him to be stricken, nor said as much as an evil word to him." Cervantes's own account is borne out by a contemporary who, in a history of Algiers written before *Don Quixote* had made its author famous, tells us that "of the captivity and brave deeds of Miguel de Cervantes one could write a whole history. Four times he narrowly avoided death by impaling, hanging, or burning for having set fellow captives free. And if fortune had aided his courage and ingenuity, Algiers would be in Christian hands today, for he aimed at no less." And indeed, while still a captive, Cervantes wrote to King Philip's secretary urging the conquest of Algiers. If only he were ransomed, he wrote, he would throw himself at the King's feet and say, "Great monarch, you who have enslaved a thousand barbarian peoples, who receive tribute even from the blacks of India, how can you tolerate the resistance of a miserable hovel? Ah, could you but complete the work begun by your valiant father!"

"Your valiant father"—always, in his heroic dreams, Cervantes, like other Spaniards, looks back to the Emperor Charles V. Later, in the preface which he wrote for his collected short stories, he gave a brief autobiographical sketch of himself, which compresses into two sentences his cult of heroism, his pride in his own heroic life, and his veneration for the Emperor. The author of these stories, he says, "was a soldier for many years, and a captive for five and a half years, and so learned patience in adversity. He lost his left hand from an arquebus-shot at the sea fight of Lepanto: an ugly wound, which, however, he thought comely because he had received it in the greatest, most memorable event that the past has seen or the future may hope to see, fighting under the triumphant banners of [Don John of Austria] the son of that thunderbolt of war, Charles V of happy memory."

Such was the Cervantes who, in 1580, returned from captivity to the Spain of Philip II. We can recognize him perfectly: he is a true, if somewhat belated, representative of the first of our two generations, the heroic, romantic, chivalrous generation of Charles V. But when he returned to Spain, what did he find? Already, while he had been breathing the heady air of Italy, fighting at Lepanto, braving his infidel captors in Algiers, the new generation was taking over

FROM *Histoire d'un Grand Livre, Don Quichotte*, 1957; COURTESY JOSEPH FORET, ED.

COURTESY ANTONIO FRASCONI

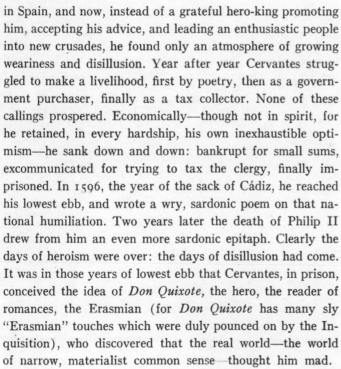

In a woodcut by the American Antonio Frasconi (above), Don Quixote charges the windmill beneath a portentous sun and star. But the last word in psychological interpretation is Salvador Dali's Don spinning in turmoil (right).

in Spain, and now, instead of a grateful hero-king promoting him, accepting his advice, and leading an enthusiastic people into new crusades, he found only an atmosphere of growing weariness and disillusion. Year after year Cervantes struggled to make a livelihood, first by poetry, then as a government purchaser, finally as a tax collector. None of these callings prospered. Economically—though not in spirit, for he retained, in every hardship, his own inexhaustible optimism—he sank down and down: bankrupt for small sums, excommunicated for trying to tax the clergy, finally imprisoned. In 1596, the year of the sack of Cádiz, he reached his lowest ebb, and wrote a wry, sardonic poem on that national humiliation. Two years later the death of Philip II drew from him an even more sardonic epitaph. Clearly the days of heroism were over: the days of disillusion had come. It was in those years of lowest ebb that Cervantes, in prison, conceived the idea of *Don Quixote,* the hero, the reader of romances, the Erasmian (for *Don Quixote* has many sly "Erasmian" touches which were duly pounced on by the Inquisition), who discovered that the real world—the world of narrow, materialist common sense—thought him mad.

For of course Don Quixote is Cervantes. This is well pointed out by one of the most perceptive writers on Spanish literature, Mr. Gerald Brenan. "I think we ought to take note," he says, "that the famous knight had many features in common with his creator. We learn, for example, that Don Quixote was of the same age as Cervantes when he set out on his adventures, and that he had the same physical appearance: we read of his wits being dry and sterile and his head turned by too much reading, just as we are told in the

preface that his author's were. Moreover, he was the incorrigible optimist and idealist who set out to reform the world by force of arms and instead was beaten by it. Must not this, or something like it, have been Cervantes's view of his own history? . . . I suggest therefore that one of the sources of Don Quixote's power to move us comes from his being a projection of a discarded part of Cervantes himself: that is to say, of the noble intentions and failure of his life. It is for this reason that the irony in this most ironical of books has often the deep and searching quality of self-irony."

No doubt it is self-irony, but also it is a delicate self-irony: that is why it is so attractive, why it makes so great a book. When a man makes steppingstones of his dead selves, he is very likely (as Samuel Butler once wrote) to jump upon them to some tune. But Cervantes did not jump. If he is disillusioned, there is nothing vindictive or cynical about his disillusion. How could there be, when half of his own life had been invested in those illusions which he now found himself, with all Spain, forced to mock? A generation would come which had made no such investment and which could afford to be severe against the fantasies of the past. But Cervantes could not, for he had a foot in either world. And so he wrote essentially not for the future (though the eighteenth century would rediscover him and set him among the immortals), but for his own generation, the generation of the disillusioned, which could yet regret its illusions: for they were its own.

H. R. Trevor-Roper, Regius Professor of Modern History at Oxford, has written frequent historical essays for HORIZON.

On Screen: SUSANNAH YORK

Rare is the actor who can make the act of eating or drinking an arresting business in itself. Charles Laughton is one (who can forget his Henry VIII of England majestically launching a chicken carcass over his shoulder?); Marlon Brando's Stanley Kowalski was a spellbinder with a beer bottle, and Brando can still talk his way around a drumstick; Wallace Beery made his way with provender a stock in trade; and there was, of course, Chaplin's immortal handling of a boiled shoe. Now, a young woman named Susannah York bites deeply into a ripe greengage plum; the camera closes in to observe the juicy fruit caught on a full and tender lip, the trickles down a dewy, innocent face; and her course toward stardom seems certain.

In *Loss of Innocence* (the American film version of Rumer Godden's novel, *The Greengage Summer*), Miss York does a good deal more than munch upon plums to justify her sudden acclaim as the most interesting young English actress to emerge in years. In an adult yet fetchingly improbable story she portrays Joss, the eldest of three English children who find themselves spending a summer in a French château occupied by this assortment: its owner, a vintage woman of the world; her Lesbian manageress; an international jewel thief out of a good English family; and a scullery boy of lustful appetites. Miss York is required to effect the metamorphosis from a sixteen-year-old schoolgirl—complete with gray uniform and tie—at summer's beginning, to a budded young creature at summer's end who provokes the scullery boy to rape and the thief to drift away from his aging mistress as he finds his cynical heart touched by the girl's beauty and sensibility.

Seldom has the bittersweet image of youth on the verge of maturity been projected so affectingly. There is her shy, searching glance into the thief's face when she senses the flicker that is his first, almost unconscious response to her femininity; there is the way she descends the staircase, with the measured movements of a girl who would be a woman. Miss York's achievement in this role affirms what her single previous film appearance had promised. In *Tunes of Glory* she had a minor part between two of England's finest actors—Alec Guinness and John Mills—playing the daughter to Sir Alec's rambunctious old soldier, the acting commander of a Highland regiment, who is superseded by a cool, Oxonian colonel (Mills). Somehow, in the shadow of these two masters, Miss York made her presence felt: fresh, unmannered, she gave thrust to a modest character. Important roles in a number of the better British television dramas followed. Since her performance of Joss scripts have come to her door. She expects to do a play in the West End later

this season, has signed a five-picture contract with the British-born producer Victor Saville, and has won the vied-for feminine lead in the film based on the life of Sigmund Freud, which John Huston is directing in Vienna from a script by Jean-Paul Sartre.

At nineteen, Susannah York has had only scant professional training. The eldest daughter of an English family settled in Scotland, she was educated at a private school, traveled on the Continent, became fluent in French, Spanish, and Italian, and entertained her sisters with plays of her own devising. For a year and a half she did attend the Royal Academy of Dramatic Art. "But I had no thought of becoming a film actress until it just sort of happened. Right until I went to RADA, going to the films was a treat. Growing up in Scotland, I mean, children just don't; movies were something that I saw at Christmastime."

Off stage, Miss York is still more girl than actress: her frocks are simple; she sits shoeless, legs tucked beneath her; her stride is coltish; her laughter sudden; her speech without artifice. Yet she has poise, taste, a measure of shrewdness, and a sense of humor. "I suppose that actresses are always acting," she says, "but I try not to, honestly. Anyhow, my family, my younger sisters, are awfully blasé about my career." And in response to a question: "We [her husband, Michael Wells, is an actor] live in a flat near Chelsea; I love big abstract pictures, and, yes, it has a view, a marvelous view—of the gasworks."

Miss York is not yet a finished actress, but her appetite for acting experience is impressive. There is a scene in *Loss of Innocence* in which Joss, her pride hurt, drinks her first champagne, lots of it, and becomes wildly tight. Though badly edited, the scene is a tour de force. "I'd never been tight," Miss York recalls, "though I do have an affinity for wine, not spirits. I told the director that I couldn't imagine how Joss felt, and I had to know. So I had ten or twelve glasses of English cider. It's quite bubbly, you know. Well, I played the scene. But, oh, my! I had to leave the set for an hour, screaming it off."

During the production of *Tunes of Glory,* she spent every possible minute watching Mills and Guinness. "It was a fantastic experience," she says. "I mean they are so professional. One thing I found especially off-putting: his, Alec's, snap way of walking from a conversation off the set right onto it and into a scene when his call came. He was *on.* I mean to say, I can't do it. I don't go all Method, but I need *something* to get me into it."

Whatever that something is, Miss York seems to find it.

ROBERT EMMETT GINNA

115

Photograph by PHILIPPE HALSMAN

On Screen: JEAN-PAUL BELMONDO

"As soon as I was dressed for the role with that hat on my head and the cigarette in the corner of my mouth, I felt at ease in the character. All I needed was a tic. Jean-Luc Godard, the director, has a habit of pinching his lower lip, and I thought I ought to do that. But I wasn't comfortable with it. Then I remembered Humphrey Bogart's gesture of rubbing a finger across his lip. I was ready to go."

Wearing the mantle of celebrity with grace at the modest age of twenty-eight, Jean-Paul Belmondo thus recalls the bare elements that helped him create a memorable Parisian punk in *Breathless (A Bout de Souffle)*, the film that catapulted him to fame upon its appearance in 1959.

The odds were heavy against the movie's success. Its original conception was meager. ("All we had to begin with was this: a guy steals a car in Marseilles, kills a cop on the road, gets to Paris where he loves a girl who doesn't love him, and dies.") A script was never written; it was improvised, often at a café table by all hands, between takes. ("We all thought the producer would go mad. For the last scene, where I die in the street—the one that caused so much comment—Godard said to me, 'Run until you've had it, then fall.' That's what I did. One take, ten minutes. A cop saw me fall and raced over; he was furious when he found out we were just making a movie.")

Not until the film was shown in Paris were its makers aware that they had hit the crest of the New Wave. Belmondo exploded out of the screen with critics raving about his "allure of nothingness, of virile cowardice." In his loose-limbed walk, his unprepossessing looks, his hard-boiled Parisian accent, and the unrestrained obscenity of his language, he incarnated the image in which an impressive part of Parisian youth sees itself—tough yet tender, inarticulate yet intelligent, outside society but superior to it; and François Mauriac, coining *le mot juste*, sadly wrote of the dawn of *Belmondisme*. Such was the impact in France of the character that Belmondo created.

The improbable place where this Gallic exponent of the Brando school of acting learned his trade was the staid Paris Conservatoire—training ground for the Comédie-Française. What business Belmondo had there, with his unclassic slouch and his even less classic features, was a matter for puzzled speculation. Plainly, his eyes were too small, his teeth too big, his mouth too wide, his lips too thick, and his nose too wavy. "With that face you'll never be able to take a girl in your arms," he was told; "the audience would split its sides laughing." He fought his teachers all the way. "They wanted me to play stiff," he says. "I wanted to play relaxed, natural. I still don't like that one-note tone of a theater that's more like a museum."

As a student, Belmondo devoted as much of his talent to horseplay as to studying the art of the theater. Even today he is apt to stop dead in the middle of the street and declaim at the top of his voice—in the tones of the Comédie-Française—the entire text of an advertising poster. His most exuberant role at the Conservatoire, which brought down the curtain as well as the house, was an impromptu Tarzan. Scratching himself gorilla-fashion and howling the call of the jungle, he raced across the stage, leaped up into the curtains, and swung from them until they tore to the stage, burying him in an immense cloud of dust that had been accumulating for decades. Appropriately, at the graduation-competition of his class he used his sense of comedy to superb effect. He did a scene from an obscure Feydeau farce with such wit that he laid the audience in the aisle. But since prize-winners normally go on to the Comédie-Française and since Belmondo's acting instrument, his face and figure, made his entry "unthinkable," the judges bypassed him. At that, the audience erupted in catcalls and hisses, and his classmates carried him across the stage on their shoulders in rebellious triumph while he acknowledged the wild acclaim of the crowd by raising his clasped hands like a victorious boxer. It was a unique exit from the austere Conservatoire. The next day the scandal was splashed across the front pages of the Paris press, and the publicity brought Belmondo his first small stage and screen roles.

Since *Breathless* he has become France's most sought-after screen actor and has made a total of nine films. (*Moderato Cantabile*, written by Marguerite Duras and directed by Peter Brook, is Belmondo's next important film due here.) His parts have been varied, testifying to his range as well as his intensity: a tender-hearted adventurer, an unrequited lover, a slap-happy photographer, an irresistible philanderer, a bespectacled intellectual, a visionary peasant, a flint-eyed killer, an amorous priest, and even a duke—a comic duke, but still a bewigged, costumed, bona fide, eighteenth-century duke.

"I don't want to repeat myself," Belmondo recently remarked. "I want to hit a different tone with every character. They said I created a new style of acting in *A Bout de Souffle*. But that style existed long before me, in the United States. I studied Garfield, Bogart, Brando, and I liked Cooper, too. That's where I went to school, where they play it relaxed." Belmondo looked dreamy. "I want to get back to the stage and someday feel ready to do Shakespeare, the big roles. But first I'd like to do a movie in the United States," he added in his rich Parisian accent, and his eyes lighted up. "What I'd like to do is a western."

BERNARD FRIZELL

SLACKMAN

TRY "*MASSACHUSETTS*" ON *YOUR* PIANO

The rich and populous state of New York has existed since 1776. It contains, reading from left to right, Niagara Falls, Howard Hanson (leading the Eastman School Symphony Orchestra), 149 species of trees, Lake Placid (headquarters of fonetik speling), Schenectady (scene of the 1690 massacre), Governor and Mrs. Rockefeller (surrounded by antique furniture, contemporary art, and future ambitions), the Hudson River, stiff skyscrapers, pliable commuters, blue jeans, white ducks, and—like an unexpected pimple on the end of a long thin nose—Montauk. It has people. It has variety. It has wealth. It has a grand past and a glorious future. But it has never had a state song.

This has worried many inhabitants of New York, but it remained for Mrs. Bessie A. Buchanan, a member of the State Assembly, to do something about it. She sat down and wrote a set of lyrics herself. And last spring her fellow Assemblymen unanimously approved, as well they might, a bill making their colleague's poem the official song of the state. It seems, however, to have run afoul of the Senate Finance Committee. While the population of New York waits to see whether the matter will be allowed to rest there, we have time to examine the poem itself.

The principal difficulty confronting any poet who attempts to write such a song is the name of the state. Short and clear, but far from euphonious, the two syllables *New York* do not lend themselves to the rhythms of exalted lyricism. They sound too much like a hoarse two-toot taxi horn or an inarticulate roar from a traffic cop. It is hard to do much more with them than the lyricists who, for Leonard Bernstein's *On the Town*, wrote

New York, New York—a hell of a town!
The Bronx is up and the Battery's down,
The people ride in a hole in the ground. . . .

The name *New York* will scarcely rhyme with anything worth using in a poem. Mrs. Buchanan has solved this problem with confident ease. Not many modern poets would have thought of breaking down the barrier of rhyme in the very first couplet, but she has done so. Her song (as reported in the New York *Times*) begins

In all the world there's no place like New York,
Where dreams come true and happy hearts are taught. . . .

That is bold. That is direct and energetic and unconventional, like New York itself. To rhyme *York* to *taught*—that is really cutting the Gordian knauck. Some contemporary

poets, for instance Auden, have used assonance all through their poems, but Mrs. Buchanan does not. In the rest of her lyric she employs conventional rhymes: *light—might, revere—dear*. But at the opening of this important poem, she clearly felt it was necessary to produce a sound-effect as daring and unique as New York State itself.

Here is the text of her entire poem:

In all the world there's no place like New York.
Where dreams come true and happy hearts are taught
To walk and work together in freedom and in light,
To make our state the greatest in progress and in might.
In every way we honor and revere
The sight and sound of all we hold so dear,
From the beauty of the mountains to the magic of streams,
And our buildings reaching high unto the sky.
In God we trust that peace will ever reign
O'er New York State, our home and proud domain.

You will notice that the ten lines are grouped into five couplets. The first couplet contains the new breakthrough rhyme *York—taught*. The second and third are regular. The fourth suddenly surges upwards into a fountain of lyricism which interrupts the sequence. Not even Mrs. Buchanan, bold though she may be, could ask us to rhyme *streams* to *sky*. Evidently she has left *streams* without a partner (and indeed, what could rival the Hudson River?), while *sky* is rhymed to the companionable word within its own line, *high*.

A carping critic might make one objection to the style of Mrs. Buchanan's poem: that, if read by itself without the music which it was designed to inspire, it concentrates rather too closely on one rhetorical device, the repetition of closely allied ideas in pairs: *walk* and *work*, *freedom* and *light*, *progress* and *might*, *honor* and *revere*, *sight* and *sound*, *home* and *domain*. Still, this is doubtless meant to image the structure of New York State, which is composed partly of a city of ten million people (with their suburban dormitories) voting to spend money, and partly of a farming and industrial area containing ten million people voting to save money. A poem often reflects the very structure of its subject.

The problem of rhythm is one which the composer must settle with the poet, for surely a lyric such as this demands music so that it may be sung and played by myriads of New York Staters. The New York *Times* in its brief report says that the song is "in march tempo." This is, on the whole, true, except for a couplet which appears to be in waltz time:

By GILBERT HIGHET

From the beauty of the mountains to the magic of the streams
And our buildings reaching high ———— unto the sky.

But perhaps that couplet is a sort of scherzo, meant for the drum majorettes to sing while turning somersaults in front of the marching bands.

The anthem closes with a noble heroic couplet:

> *In God we trust that peace will ever reign*
> *O'er New York State, our home and proud domain.*

The problem of fitting the three hard syllables *New York State* into an iambic line has at last been solved. Mrs. Buchanan has hammered them in, and they will stay in.

With her stirring song, Mrs. Buchanan has at last put New York on the same level as many other states, some of them less populous, less ambitious, and less plentifully supplied with literary talent. There are a few which have resisted the temptation—or, perhaps we might say, have been deprived of the opportunity—of having their own state song. Massachusetts, for example, faces a virtually insoluble problem. If it is ever to have its name introduced into poetry, either the traditional rhyme schemes of American-English literature will have to be abandoned or the poem will be written in Algonquian. Vermont has been too thrifty, New Jersey too busy, and North Dakota too cold to have acquired state songs. Some of the southern states have contented themselves with the famous old traditional songs, *My Old K Home, Carry Me back to Old V,* and so forth. Mississippi has no official song, but it has a state ode, ending in phrases worthy of Faulkner's necrophilic Miss Emily:

> *Here, my life, ebb thou away;*
> *Here, my bones, turn back to clay—*
> *I love thee, Mississippi.*

Other states have had their own songs written and officially approved long ago. One of the most stirring is the Alabama song, by Julia S. Tutwiler. This is only a sample of its lyricism:

> *Broad the Stream whose name thou bearest;*
> *Grand thy Bigbee rolls along;*
> *Fair thy Coosa—Tallapoosa*
> *Bold thy Warrior, dark and strong,*
> *Goodlier than the land that Moses*
> *Climbed lone Nebo's Mount to see,*
> *Alabama, Alabama,*
> *We will aye be true to thee!*

With its combination of southern scenery and Biblical tradition, this hymn would be difficult to excel. In a young state, sentiments are naturally simpler:

> *Montana, Montana, Glory of the West*
> *Of all the states from coast to coast*
> *You're easily the best—*
> *Montana, Montana,*
> *Where skies are always blue*
> *M-O-N-T-A-N-A, Mon-ta-na, I love you.*

West Virginia, on the other hand, found in Mrs. Ellen King a poet who could not only eulogize the principal features of her landscape but actually image them in the antiphonal setting of the state hymn:

> *O the hills   beautiful hills*
> *beautiful hills   beautiful hills*
> *How I love those West Virginia hills.*
> *If o'er sea or land I roam*
> *Still I'll think of happy home,*
> *And the friends among the West Virginia hills.*

Mrs. Harriet Parker Camden of Oklahoma could hardly foresee in 1905, that her state would be definitively glorified by two native New Yorkers thirty-eight years later, but she did her best in a sort of Student Prince song:

> *We have often sung her praises,*
> *But we have not told the half,*
> *So I give you "Oklahoma,"*
> *'Tis a toast we all can quaff.*

But this was perhaps too sophisticated for a state which was nominally dry until 1959, and has probably been superseded by the simple song in which the entire company faces the audience, and the entire audience faces the company, and both join in a big locomotive, O-O-O-O-O-O-Oklahoma!

Among the most recent of the official poets is Roger Vinton Snow, who in 1932 created a song for the State of Maine, containing a group of clichés aged in the wood:

> *Oh Pine Tree State*
> *Your woods, fields and hills*
> *Your lakes, streams and rock-bound coast*
> *Will ever fill our hearts with thrills*
> *And tho' we seek far and wide our search will be in vain*
> *To find a fairer spot on earth than*
> *(cresc.) Maine!*
> *(in strict tempo) Maine! Maine!*

At the next Presidential inauguration, it would be a fine thing if they abolished the songs of love and laudation sung to the embarrassed wives of the new President and Vice-President. (Remember *Jac–que–line,* which is not even how the First Lady pronounces her name? and the marvelous phrase "she studies books"?) Instead, the separate delegations might send choruses to sing the songs of their states.

> *And here we have I–da–ho*
> *Winning her way to fame*
> *Silver and gold in the sunlight blaze,*
> *And romance lies in her name. . . .*

Soon after that would come *Iowa—"Beautiful Land,"* written by a poet named Tacitus Hussey, of Des Moines; and then, toward the end, poor in grammar but unimpeachable in sentiment:

> *Wyoming, Wyoming, Precious art thou and thine;*
> *Wyoming, Wyoming, Beloved state of mine!*

So far we have seen only one single verse—or perhaps it may be a chorus?—of the proposed New York state song. Surely it will not be permitted to fall below the level of the other states? Twenty million hopeful New Yorkers look toward Mrs. Bessie A. Buchanan, and ask her for more.

LA DOLCE VIA

In America a street is only a way,

while in Italy it is a way of life

By JAMES MARSTON FITCH

Old Mrs. Trollope, that indefatigable writer of last century's travel books, observed with her usual bluntness that Italian streets were safe for no one but Italians: the foreigner, in dodging the carriages which raced down the narrow streets, was apt to be run down by pedestrians. Things have not changed much since her day. Even now the Italians bring to the management of their street life a sort of Alice-in-Wonderland logic that leaves the American—accustomed, as he likes to think, to traffic hazards—feeling like a choir boy in the midst of a football scrimmage. There may be rules of play, but he has no chance to learn them. The signals are all in a foreign tongue and, in side-stepping one player, he gets hit by three others. He ends in the mud every time.

To master the Italian street it is necessary first to understand that it is the exact reverse of the American. It seems inscrutable, where ours is immediately legible; closed, where ours appears to be open; inhospitable, where ours (with its glass fronts, fenceless lawns, and picture windows) seems to invite full and free inspection of merchandise and family life alike. The impression of reserve, secrecy, even hostility, is a function of the very construction of the Italian street. Instead of the light, skeletal architecture of America, arranged in forthright gridirons, the Italian street is lined with heavy load-bearing masonry, with barred and shuttered windows and cavernous arcades. Even in the newer parts of town, where the streets broaden out with proper curbs and sidewalks, where houses sit back in gardens—even here, high walls topped with savage bits of broken bottles and pierced by locked gates maintain a first impression of inhospitality.

All this may be true. But it does not alter the fact that the American street is, by and large, the coldest and loneliest landscape this side of Mars, while the Italian street affords the most delicious experience of embrace and enclosure of any space on earth. The American street is mere process, a means of getting from where you are to where you want to be. Nothing ever happens there: you may see life but only as you do in an aquarium, behind glass. The Italian street, on the other hand, is the actual stage of life itself. Business, courting, visiting, dining, politics, and tasks that are

portable—all these acts transpire here in the street or as close to its margins as local weather and topography permit. The very weekends and holidays that make graveyards of American cities bring everyone in Italy into town. Then the streets will be bubbling with people luxuriating in their escape from too-open country skies, relaxing in spaces snugly defined by patterned pavements, open shop fronts, and tidy barbered trees. Merely to move about in such spaces is to enjoy a kind of public wealth which, in some pervasive way, compensates for the private poverty of so many Italians. Better than most, they understand what a splendid gift to men a city is.

Venice has many small squares and busy quays (the latter are called—with exquisite appropriateness in that aqueous environment—*fondamente*): to enter them is like stepping onto the stage of a Mozart opera. The crowds are lucky to be in spaces so flattering to human activity and they know it. They inhabit these vehicle-free pavements so completely and artistically that it is hard for the tourist to believe that they are hard-working Venetians and not extras engaged for the occasion. And in Florence there is a certain downtown block which, for centuries, was the locus of a cattle mart. It has been many years since the last white cow was led into this area, slipping on the cobbles and soiling them with her nervous stool. But the market still takes place there. On stated days traffic is diverted and the farmers appear, filling the street from wall to wall and converting it into a wonderful roofless hall, vibrant with masculine activity and warm on the coldest day. And in every Italian town you will find piazzas and enclaves inhabited by such venerable institutions. Real as granite, invisible as air, they reappear on certain dates (written nowhere, known to all) to occupy these spaces as the hand does the glove.

The Italians often seem to be more at ease in the street than in their homes. And little wonder: the street is actually more comfortable, much of the time, than the inside of many Italian houses. There are always sunny, wind-free nooks and rainproof loggias when cold weather and the high cost of fuel combine to render the rooms of most people extremely uncomfortable. Besides, in terms of modern conveniences, the street is often better equipped than the house. There is always fresh running water here—in the poorest quarters, often the only water. It is usually dispensed in handsome fountains, where children can wade while mothers sew; or in utilitarian wash houses, where the women can visit while doing the family wash. The street has airy *pissoirs* for the men and public toilets for both sexes. (These latter are not always as clean as Americans might demand, and here they have not yet unraveled the secret of toilet paper. But there are many more of them than any American town affords; and the scribbling on the walls is more often a call to political action than to sexual deviation.) In the larger towns such sanitary facilities are expanded into the *albergo diurno*, a public enclave off the public street that serves most of the needs and emergencies the body is heir to. This Italian institution, though it may be but a dwarfed and dwindled descendant of the great Roman thermae, is still a much more comprehensive service to human frailty than any public bath in Northern Europe or America. Here, attended by friendly and sympathetic slatterns, one can purchase pedicures, showers, aspirins, enemas, haircuts, or letter paper. Warm and steamy, the atmosphere combines the most en-

dearing aspects of the country doctor's office and the neighborhood bordello.

The American street, with its open ends and straight, impervious walls, acts like a sluice for both pedestrian and vehicular traffic. The result is a riptide along the face of the buildings that makes street life impossible. The Italian street is structured quite otherwise. Seldom straight and never open-ended, it is lined with buildings whose very irregularity of plan and profile creates a wide range of nooks, re-entrant angles, and cul-de-sacs. These, like the verges of a quiet stream, provide the necessary conditions for many kinds of street life. This life, moreover, expands and contracts with the season, with the day of the week, with the very hour of the day. A spot that is choice in December will be deserted in July. The center of gravity of each piazza will shift hourly as the sun moves. On a blazing summer afternoon in Venice, when shade is at a premium, the shadow of a flagstaff in the Piazza San Marco will be just wide enough to accommodate a line of pigeons, strung like beads along its length and moving as it moves. A restaurant in Naples retreats into its shadowy grottoes from lunch through siesta; but once in shadow, it will move out onto the street like a snail from its shell. The waiters—with a few potted privets, some rugs, and a bridge lamp or two—will create a full sense of enclosure in what was only empty pavement a few moments before.

Beneath these balanced movements of advance and retreat exists an intricate system of accommodation, nepotism, and petty bribery of municipal officials. The butcher has no right to hang his bloody carcasses outside his shop. The vendors of chestnuts and cooked tripe, the flower sellers and blind lottery-ticket peddlers, have no legal authority to block this bit of sidewalk or that friendly angle of wall. But these are

venial sins in Italian eyes, understood and overlooked in return for the urban amenity they yield.

All this ebb and flow of life tends to obliterate the curb line, that strict demarcation between sidewalk and street, pedestrian and traffic, which is the iron law of survival in America. Often there are no sidewalks at all, so that there could be no strict separation of foot and wheeled traffic even if the Italians wanted it. But there is ample evidence that they do not want it. Even in those newer sections where there are proper sidewalks for pedestrians and curbs for the dogs, people still take to the streets. They will stroll mildly down the very center, especially if it is Sunday or spring or if they are young mothers with perambulators. The cause of such behavior is clearly not one of curbs and sidewalks but of national attitudes. The streets *belong* to them, and their street manners spring from this important fact. This is the scene of their outside, their social, world—the obverse of that family life which seems so cloistered and antisocial to the outsider. This is where the sexes mix on terms more nearly equal than indoors. This is where children escape the strict discipline of school and home. This is where men meet men and women escape momentarily the drudgery of housework in a land of expensive soap, scarce fuel, and unbelievably hard water.

Color and movement inevitably result from all this activity, yet it is anything but the picture of idle ease so dear to the operetta. On the contrary, this is the color and movement of a people intent upon tasks requiring hard work, close attention, and much skill. (There is, of course, some authentic idling in the cafés along the Via Veneto or in the Galleria in Milan; but oftener than not these loungers will turn out to be either tourists or locals who make their living off tourists. Most Italians take their espresso indoors, where

Drawings by NICHOLAS SOLOVIOFF

service is quicker and prices 50 per cent lower.) In the working-class streets, everybody is working—men, women, children. In the villages, the animals are also at work— horses, donkeys, oxen. The shepherd's dog wears an air of social usefulness, and the busy cackle of the hens shows that they, too, are aware of adding to the general welfare. Even the village cats seem businesslike, mixing pleasure with rat-catching. In the afternoon, in sun or shade as season dictates, the women gather to gossip. But underneath the gossip, handwork of almost ferocious intensity is carried forward— the sewing and strawwork of the cottage industries. This underpaid labor is farmed out everywhere: along country lanes you will see young girls or old women minding a few goats or a treasured pig. Even they will be plaiting straw braid as they walk. The Italian streetscape is dyed with the colors of real work.

And much of this street work is, of course, the traffic itself. Italian streets, like streets everywhere, are being inundated by automobiles. This conflict between the wheel and the foot is not new to the Peninsula—even in Augustan Rome it was so severe that heavy carting could only be done at night—but it has reached an acute stage. Even so, the Italian pedestrians have not abdicated their rights to the pavement as the Americans have; daily they fight for it, millimeter by millimeter. Moreover, native taste and local necessity have combined to produce automobiles less night-marish in size and profile than the American ones. Indeed, egged on by the high price of steel and gasoline, Italian designers have produced some of the smallest gasoline-powered vehicles on earth: the tiny Fiats, the sway-backed Lambrettas and Vespas, and bicycle motors so small that they hide behind the sprocket and can be filled with an eyedropper (and so weak, one must add, that on a hill both motor and cyclist work, making it difficult to tell who is helping whom).

But most of Italy's wheeled traffic is still unmotorized. The horse, the donkey, and—in the villages and the countryside—the ox still pull most of the loads. These draft animals add color to all but the largest cities: the pleasant liquid ring of the horses' hoofs on pavement and the dainty tinkle of the donkeys'; furry little ponies hardly larger than shepherd dogs; classic white oxen with bottomless brown eyes and unbelievable eyelashes; mauve donkeys with the stripes of zebra ancestors still faintly traceable on their delicate legs. All these picturesque animals move along at their traditional pace—except when there is an occasional burst of speed from one of the shabbily elegant carriages that still cruise the streets. These come careening toward you, their iron tires setting up a fearful clatter and the driver brandishing his whip so alarmingly that your best hope of safety is, as James Fenimore Cooper once advised, to flag it down and climb aboard.

Since human labor is still the cheapest form of energy in Italy, the streets are filled with every sort of pushcart, pedicab, and bicycle. The bicycles! The rest of the world has a thing or two to learn from the Italians here. They can carry almost anything in their handle-bar baskets—briefcases, babies, marketing, friends. Hunters set off for the mountains with their dogs up there, expectantly sniffing the morning air. Even the street cleaners and garbage collectors move about on bicycles. And these are not the fat, chrome-laden machines of the U.S.A. They are instead fined down to a lean and racy line. Most cyclists are lean and racy, too.

They weave in and out of traffic like swallows, taking openings any bird would flinch at and (like birds again) whistling their warnings instead of ringing their bells. (The perennial favorite seems to be a bar or two from Chaplin's *Limelight* music.) When two friends meet they will peddle slowly along, side by side in the middle of the street, as intent upon their conversation as if they were seated in a café. If one of them happens to be motorized, the other will hitch a ride by placing a cupped hand on the friend's shoulder in a gesture both comradely and energy-saving, and the little motor will pull them both along.

These are the main elements of Italian traffic. All of them—mechanical, animal, and human—are on the street at the same time and in the same place. There is a pattern to their movement, though it may not always be apparent to the outsider. Nominally, traffic moves on the right-hand side though in real life it moves on all sides. The standard location of the steering wheel is on the left, but the bigger cars can be had with either left- or right-hand drive. In addition, many of the big trucks and buses have right-hand drive, as do, of course, the horse cabs and dray carts. As a consequence, the Italian attitude toward right and left is ambivalent, and there is no concept of "giving way," as the English put it, to the party on one's right. There is, indeed, no concept of giving way at all. Except for the downtown sections of the larger cities, disciplined by signal lights and white-helmeted *vigili,* an intersection becomes for each person a test of wits, courage, and timing. Precedence goes not to the right but to the bold.

This code of manners extends even to the canals of Venice, where boat traffic behaves with the same unnerving anarchy. Here, in fact, you see Italian behavior at its most dramatic, most fluid moment. The swift and silent gondolas shoot out of the cross-canals without warning, aimed (or so it seems to the tourist) directly at his boat. Apparently, there is never a collision, the miss being narrow but very graceful. But then a big cabin cruiser will come roaring down the Grand Canal; or one of the low-slung powerful boats of the fire department will come careening around some watery corner, sirens going full tilt. There is no time to head for shelter. The gondolas all freeze like ducks in a pond while the big boat goes roaring by, threatening to capsize everything it does not hit. The gondoliers all curse softly under their breath; the Venetian passengers stand up and balance themselves like Canadian logrollers in a spring freshet; the tourists cling grimly to the gunwales; and the wavelets lap wickedly at the eroding foundations of the old *palazzi.*

In town and country, motor traffic moves with great dash and style. The Italian seems always to be a skillful driver, but his bland confidence in brakes and luck is enough to chill the blood. Overtaking and passing all cars on the highway seems to be, for him, a matter of face. Thus passing on blind curves or hilltops becomes the rule rather than the exception, since the roads are mostly one or the other. And this technique is extended right down into the central districts, where cars, trucks, and scooters weave through the crowds with the baroque grace of Bernini. Yet, despite this driving, the pedestrians do not leap to one side as you might expect. Often in these narrow sidewalkless streets there is no place to leap to. But even when there is, the Italian pedestrian invariably looks around, before giving way, as if to make sure there really *is* a car behind him.

For the American tourist, accustomed to the miserable status of a stateless person on the streets at home, such confidence is heartwarming. But let you drive a car along these same streets and the problem shows another face. For then it is apparent that these same pedestrians seem not to have even a Stone Age understanding of what damage a moving car can wreak on frail human flesh. They seem to regard it as nothing better than an equal, stepping out of its way like a bullfighter, pulling in the hips with elegant timing—not an instant too soon, not a millimeter too far. Often, when your car is brought to a halt, they will steady themselves against your fender as they pass by. Or again, if heavy traffic slows you down to their pace, they will walk along beside your car with one hand on the window sill, much as they might help you across the room to a chair.

No one, whether afoot or driving, looks where he is going. Or, to put it more precisely, everyone looks *only* where he is going, straight ahead, like a daydreamer or a sleepwalker. In fact, the more you drive on them, the more somnambulistic the Italian streets appear. Everyone is so intent upon his own affairs, his attention so focused upon his own interior world, that to blow a horn at him seems a rude invasion of his privacy. Motorists and cyclists alike will come wheeling around a blind corner, on your side of the street, to stop only inches away from your windshield. And the surprise upon their faces at seeing you is that of one startled from a deep sleep. Your being just there, at just that time, is a contingency upon which no one, apparently, had counted.

This inward-turning vision also explains the traffic jams which offer both inconvenience and diversion to the passerby. In such crooked and narrow streets any incident, however petty, can cause a bottleneck. Immediately some im-

patient motorist will pull out to bull his way through on the wrong side of the street, only to meet another motorist coming toward him. Neither one stops, neither gives way, and both move confidently forward—thus guaranteeing a jam where one was only threatened before. Now the cars will be slowly and (one must admit it) skillfully jockeyed past one another with not a paint thickness to spare. Pedestrians pull in their stomachs and flatten themselves against the wall to watch the maneuvers. There is always one of them who will step out into the street to direct the drivers, gesturing with the eloquence of an orchestra leader which way to cut the wheels, how much, and when. The stalled cars behind the two principals maintain an air of patient and decorous interest. Sooner or later traffic moves again.

Yet the Italian motorist is not careless with his car. No one, excepting possibly the Englishman, keeps his vehicle in more immaculate condition. Like the Englishman, he does his own repair work and does it with the obvious relish of a sportsman oiling his rifle or fishing reel. The car is an instrument of pleasure; and when he drives it full out, as fast and noisily as it will go, he is not consciously taking chances. He is merely acting as though the laws of chance do not, for him, exist. Accidents occur, of course. The papers are full of them after a weekend. When they do occur, tempers are lost, voices raised, and crowds collected just as elsewhere in the world. The crowds are usually partisan, and it is not at all unusual for the enraged principals to stalk away, leaving the controversy in the hands of witnesses who take up without a dropped syllable where the principals leave off. The police are often late in arriving at the scene. And once there, they act more like umpires than cops, following the course of the argument as spectators at

a tennis match follow the course of the ball. Their function seems more one of guaranteeing the fullest and freest discussion than of making out a summons or getting traffic moving again. This does not seem strange to the Italian, who shows none of the fawning obsequiousness toward traffic cops which marks the behavior of the American. On the contrary, one often sees him arguing against the threatened ticket with Latin emphasis and often succeeding in convincing the officer of the urgency if not the justice of his cause.

Sometimes, if one is to believe the press, the police do not arrive at the scene of the accident at all. The Florentine papers, for example, gave this account of an accident in which one car rammed the rear end of another: "The respective drivers grew heated, each claiming that he was in the right, and the two automobiles remained rooted in the spot, as if they held a strategic position in the verbal battle that flamed around them." Since it was the noon rush hour, and since the accident had occurred athwart two of the most important trolley tracks in town, two lines of crowded trams began to pile up around them.

"The passengers, delayed, got out to see what the matter was," the account continued. "Meanwhile, the two drivers, wrong or right, showed no intention of moving their autos. Somebody sent a young lad on a bicycle to call a traffic policeman, the one who is always stationed in Piazza San Marco. In five minutes, with his arrival, all should have been systematized. Five, ten, twenty minutes passed, trolleys had backed up right to San Marco, but the police did not arrive.

"Then it was learned that the policeman who had been summoned by the young lad had said that regulations forbade his leaving his assigned position. The irritation of the crowd became uncontainably indignant when it was learned that the summoned policeman was not the one assigned to traffic direction but rather the other one who is placed solely to observe his colleague assigned to the intersection." Things might have really got out of hand, the story hinted, had it not been for the fortunate arrival of "the controller of trams, who gave his permission for the transfer of passengers.

"The trams were already preparing to reverse their courses, switching trolleys, conductors, and tracks, when the drivers (the damage to whose cars could not have exceeded a couple of thousand-lire notes) finally decided to abandon the field. Everyone then departed for his proper destination."

This spectacle of hundreds of Italians permitting themselves to be seriously inconvenienced by an argument involving only two of them is characteristic of their street behavior and—from their point of view—logically unassailable. Life is hard and earnest and requires the vehement defense of one's own interests by one's self. Every Italian understands that there is no help in the law and that even God helps only those who help themselves. Yet, such is the alchemy of their personality that this attitude does not produce the frozen and embarrassed impersonality of American street manners. It results instead in a kind of glowing charity toward human frailty, a heart-warming tolerance toward personal idiosyncrasy. It is an individualistic philosophy which, even in the hands of pedestrians, makes American pretensions in the field seem dwarfed and mousy by comparison: in the hands of the motorist it may be raised to the level of the irrational or perverse. Yet the street life that survived the chariots of Augustus is apt to outlive the autos of Turin and Detroit. Certainly, it offers a safer model for the human habitat than the throughways, cloverleafs, and asphalt-desert shopping centers of North America.